USER-FRIENDLY GREEK

A COMMON SENSE

APPROACH TO THE GREEK

NEW TESTAMENT

BROADMAN
& HOLMAN
PUBLISHERS

NASHVILLE, TENNESSEE

KENDELL H. EASLEY

4210-43
0-8054-1043-0

Dewey Decimal Classification: 225.48
Subject Heading: BIBLE, NEW TESTAMENT /
GREEK LANGUAGE
Library of Congress Card Catalog Number: 93-33580

Library of Congress Cataloging-in-Publication Data
Easley, Kendell H., 1949–
    User-friendly Greek : a commonsense approach
to the Greek New Testament / Kendell H. Easley.
        p.   cm.
    Includes bibliographical references and index.
    ISBN 0-8054-1043-0
    1. Greek language, biblical—grammar.   2. Bible. N.T.
    —Language, style.
    I. Title.
PA817.E27   1994
484'.4—dc20   93-33580
                                                CIP

To Nancy—
faithful and loving wife,
godly Christian woman,
partner in ministry—
who lovingly advised me to
"keep the cookies on the lowest shelf"
when I first began to teach Greek.

Contents

Preface

Much of my professional ministry as a college and seminary teacher has involved teaching students New Testament Greek. I love Greek, and I love teaching Greek. After teaching for several years, I discovered that most of my former students—overwhelmed with the time demands of ministry—had let their Greek "rust out." What they had worked aggressively and diligently in the classroom to master was laid aside. Apparently, my labors in the Greek classroom had been wasted on these students.

Is there a way to help those who study Greek to bridge the gap between formal classroom study of Greek and effective use of Greek in ministry? I have been unable to find anything in print that is both easy to use and practical, but I am persuaded that the answer ought to be a resounding yes. My personal answer is this book.

Many thanks are due the individuals involved in helping me make this book a reality. Rather than naming individuals, however, I want to mention schools. I am grateful to John Brown University, Trinity Evangelical Divinity School, and Southwestern Baptist Theological Seminary for providing the programs and the professors for their students to study New Testament Greek. These schools taught me both to know and to love Greek. I am also grateful to Toccoa Falls College and to Mid-America Baptist Theological Seminary for giving me the opportunity to teach Greek.

I especially appreciate all my intermediate Greek students, who served as guinea pigs while I was developing the contents of this book. These students encouraged me to pursue a user-friendly approach to Greek rather than a technical one. It took several student generations before I was confident enough of my approach and content to offer it to a publisher. I am grateful for the editors at Broadman & Holman Publishers, who saw in my work something that could help many people become more comfortable using their Greek. I also thank those who read all or part of the manuscript and offered valuable suggestions.

This book is offered as a sacrifice of praise to Jesus Christ the Lord. If the Greek Testament is better interpreted and proclaimed because this book is put into practice, then Christ will be lifted up. Only if He receives glory will my efforts be truly valuable.

Introduction

Many students who have completed at least a year of Greek study in college or seminary have never used their Greek in any effective way, despite their good intentions. Either they have never learned that Greek is their friend, or Greek has simply been crowded out of their schedule. If you find yourself in this category of people, this book is for you.

I wrote this book to help you use Greek regularly and effectively as you prepare to preach or teach from the New Testament. This book will not teach you everything you should know about Greek. It concentrates instead on matters that are likely to bear fruit in sermon preparation. I have included full explanations in plain English along with translated examples from the Greek Testament. Therefore, this book should be useful as a textbook for college or seminary students who are interested in the practical benefits of knowing and using Greek.

Let me offer a plan for getting the maximum benefit from this book.

1. Set aside enough time to read through an entire chapter in one sitting. Use a highlighter as you read. To be on the safe side, allow about an hour for each chapter.

2. In your next session with the book, take half an hour to an hour to work on the "Now Let's Apply!" exercise for the chapter that you previously read. Only after you have spent time working on the exercise should you turn to the Answer Key in the back of the book.

3. After you have completed the exercise, take another half-hour to re-read the chapter, just to be sure that you have a good grasp of the material.

4. When you have finished all chapters, put tabs in the book to mark the important summary tables and charts. You will return to them again and again—for example, the "Summary of Verb Tense" (pp. 56–57). Learn to keep the book next to your Greek Testament in your study or office.

Throughout the book, I have consistently used certain devices in the user-friendly part of my approach. Definitions found in the glossary appear in boldface type in the text. (The glossary will keep you from having to fumble through the book looking for something you need to know.)

I assume that readers of this book have completed a year of Greek study. You should refer to your elementary Greek textbook or to a resource such as William MacDonald's *Greek Enchiridion* to refresh your memory of paradigms and other matters of form.

If you digest the contents of this book you will accomplish two results. First, Greek will become your lifetime friend for ministry. Second, you will have a plan for using Greek simply and efficiently as you prepare to minister the Word of God.

1

From Words to Paragraphs

Biblical Greek is either a friend or a foe for ministry. For those afraid of it or ignorant of it, Greek is a foe. The major purpose of this book is to convince you that Greek can become a welcome friend. If you learn to follow a few simple steps, you will be able to handle Greek responsibly.

During my first two years of Greek study, it was hard to see where it was all heading. I was so involved in studying the individual trees that I could see little, if any, of the forest. I was bogged down trying to determine whether this verb was **iterative imperfect** or that noun was **subjective genitive**. To know exactly how these distinctions mattered or whether they could help in my sermon preparation was almost impossible.

Many students of Greek never make their way past the individual trees. After finishing formal studies, they use Greek in fits and starts, finally giving up—maybe doing a word study here or there for conscience's sake. Some preachers do study isolated Greek words as a basis for sermon preparation. This is good. A few have labored to understand the sentence structure of a verse selected for a sermon. This is better. Very few, however, have learned to go beyond the sentence level to consider a whole paragraph. This is by far the best.

As we will see, a single word has no meaning until it is put into a sentence context. In the same way, a single sentence only has meaning potential until it is placed in a paragraph context. Few sentences are logically independent. If you want to be a credible preacher, you will learn to think paragraphs.

In this chapter I want to present a sense of perspective for the whole Greek language enterprise. Let us begin by studying how the Greek language flowed. We will start with the smallest unit of the language and move outward.

1.1. The Word

Professional grammarians cannot agree on exactly what a word is, whether for English or Greek. We understand intuitively more or less what is meant by a word. In fact, learning to manage words (correctly applying prefixes, endings, and so on) is what elementary Greek classes are mainly about. You probably never defined what you meant by *word* in your Greek classes.

1.1.1. Symbol and Meaning

Let's be more specific. First, by *word* we could mean a specific series of speech sounds or the symbolic representation of speech sounds. For example, a certain speech sequence in English happens to be spelled *i-c-e*. It could have been spelled some other way: *a-i-s* or *e-y-c-e*. As far as we know this speech sequence was spelled ε-ι-ς in Greek. Of course εἰς could have been spelled differently: α-ι-ς, for instance. Both the sound sequence and the spelling sequence were arbitrary; what matters is the meaning behind the spoken or written word. (Since our interest in New Testament Greek is limited to written words, we can drop discussion of Greek speech at this point.)

By *word* I might also have in mind the meaning or sense behind the written word. Thus, when I see or hear the English word *ice*, I think of frozen water. Writers want to communicate meaning. The written marks are arbitrary symbols by which meaning is communicated. When you see the Greek word εἰς, the meaning "into" probably comes to your mind, something quite different than frozen water.

Of course other ideas are also possible for the English noun *ice*. You might think of a diamond, as in the sentence, "That three-carat piece of ice set me back thirty grand." (A different dictionary word entirely—or **lexical entry**—is the verb *ice*, as in "Did you ice that cake?") All this simply reminds us that words often carry more than one meaning. Without a context, *ice* has a range of possible meanings. (If only one meaning comes to most people's minds when they see a written word with no context, such as "frozen water" for *ice*, this is called the **unmarked meaning**.)

The Greek word εἰς has a range of meanings. It does not inherently mean "into," though this is its unmarked meaning. Before an infinitive, εἰς means "in order to", and it also has other meanings. The range of possible meanings for εἰς is extensive. Only when a speaker or writer used εἰς in a specific context did it have a specific meaning. When you first started memorizing Greek vocabulary, you were learning only unmarked meanings and not necessarily the meaning in a given context. (If you want to learn more about this, turn to section 6.5.)

Furthermore, a **lexical entry** often combines several syntactical words (various spellings). This is true both in Greek and in English. For example, the English verb *ice* exists as other syntactical words: *iced, ices, icing.* We are intuitively aware that these are different forms of the same word, but it helps to be reminded of this.

Although we have not defined *word* from a Greek point of view, we have learned four important things about words.

1.   A word is a spoken or written symbol like εἰς.

2.   At a more important level, a word is the limited set of meaning possibilities connected to a spoken or written symbol. A Greek dictionary alerts us to the range of meanings for a given word.

3.   Even more important, every word has a specific meaning in a specific context. Until we put the word *ice* into a context—a spoken or written utterance—it only has meaning potential. This observation becomes crucial when we grapple with how to do word studies. (Consider the statement, "That three-carat piece of ice set me back thirty grand." If *ice* is understood as frozen water, this sentence is absurd.)

4.   A **lexical entry** often is made up of more than one **syntactical word**. Our discussion will focus on lexical entries—the words you find listed in a standard Greek lexicon.

1.1.2. Parts of Speech

A good part of English grammar focuses on learning about parts of speech, and traditional Greek grammar has emphasized the same thing. Knowledge of parts of speech is not an end in itself. These simply provide grammatical terms for talking about language.

Again, a bit of review is in order.

1.1.2.1. The verb group. Four parts of speech belong to the Greek verb group. By far the most important part of speech is the verb itself. Basically a verb is an action word, such as ἔρχομαι (I come). A word that describes a verb is an adverb, such as καλῶς (well). A word that joins verbs or other grammatical equals is a conjunction, such as καί (and). Short words that intensify speech in various ways are called particles, such as γέ (indeed).

1.1.2.2. The noun group. Four parts of speech also belong to the noun group. The most important is the noun itself, naming a person, place, or thing, such as πατήρ (father). A word that describes a noun is an adjective, such as πιστός (faithful). The most frequent adjective is the article: ὁ, ἡ, τό (the). A word that substitutes for a noun is a pronoun, such as ἐμαυτοῦ (myself). (The noun referred to by a pronoun is its antecedent.) A word showing the relationship of a noun or pronoun to the rest of a sentence is a preposition, such as ἀντί (instead of).

1.1.3. Parts of a Word

The basic meaning component of a word has traditionally been called the **stem**. A meaning component placed before the stem is called the **prefix**; more than one prefix in a word is possible. A component placed after the stem is the **suffix**. More than one suffix in a word is frequent. A **compound word** has two stems pushed together. Modern linguistics refers to a word part as a **morpheme**; any word or part of a word that conveys some meaning is a morpheme. Consider the following examples.

1. ἐλπίζω (verb)—stem: ἐλπίζ- (hope) + suffix: -ω (present, active, indicative, first, singular) = I hope.

2. κακοποιός (noun)—stem: κακο- (bad) + stem: -ποι- (do) + suffix: -ός (masculine, nominative, singular) = evil doer.

3. ἀνόμως (adverb)—prefix: ἀ- (not) + stem: -νομ- (law) + suffix: -ως (adverb) = lawlessly.

To be able to talk about the parts of a word is helpful. Commentators have a habit of doing this. Notice how this fits into our discussion of symbol and meaning. For example, the suffix -ω can mean several different things. Only in the context of a verb stem—and then not always—does it mean present, active, indicative, first, singular. Only in the context of an entire sentence or paragraph can we be sure. On the other hand -ω does not have an unlimited range of meanings. (Just as in English, *pro-* often means "before," but not in the word *pronounce.*)

1.2. The Sentence

In English grammar classes, you learned that a sentence is a word or group of words expressing a complete thought. So it is in Greek. One-word sentences are rare in Greek, as in English. As far as we know, first-century Greek was rarely if ever written with punctuation marks, and the sentence breaks we now use are open to question at some points. Printed editions of the Greek Testament include reference information where sentence breaks are debated.

It you have studied intermediate Greek, you will remember that understanding sentences is the traditional concern of second-year Greek, just as elementary Greek focuses on learning about words. Our review of sentences begins with an examination of the three ways that words in Greek sentences can be organized.

1.2.1. Organizing Words in a Sentence

When you learned English sentence structure, you learned about four structural types of sentences: the **simple sentence**, the **compound sentence**, the **complex sentence**, and the **compound-complex sentence**. Greek sentences may be organized into the same four groups, but it is even more helpful to consider the three major ways that words in a Greek sentence can be arranged.

1.2.1.1. Main clause. A group of words that can stand alone and that contains a verb is a main clause. (Sometimes a "be" verb is only implied in the Greek text.) Any sentence with only one main clause, with or without prepositional phrases, is a simple sentence. Any sentence with two or more main clauses, with or without prepositional phrases, and without dependent clauses, is a compound sentence.

> SIMPLE: τὸ λοιπόν, ἀδελφοί μου, χαίρετε ἐν κυρίῳ.

> Finally, my brothers, rejoice in the Lord
> (Phil. 3:1).

COMPOUND: εἰς τὰ ἴδια ἦλθεν, καὶ οἱ ἴδιοι αὐτὸν οὐ παρέλαβον.

> He came to his own, and his own did not welcome him
> (John 1:11).

1.2.1.2. Prepositional phrase. This is a group of words preceded by a preposition and without a finite verb. (Greek finite verbs are indicative, subjunctive, optative, and imperative.) Prepositional phrases can be found at the beginning, end, or anywhere else in a clause, whether main or dependent. You are familiar with these from long practice in English. For preaching purposes it is important to identify prepositional phrases and separate them from the clause that they are part of.

1.2.1.3. Dependent clause. A group of words that cannot stand alone and that contains a verb is a dependent clause. In Greek, only four formats exist for dependent clauses. Each of the four formats is dominated by a particular grammatical construction.

> **1. A participle clause** is a dependent clause beginning with a participle; for example, ὁ βλέπων τοὺς δούλους (the person who sees the slaves).

> **2. An infinitive clause** is a dependent clause beginning with an infinitive; for example, βλέπειν τοὺς δούλους (to see the slaves).

> **3. A subordinate conjunction clause** is a dependent clause beginning with a subordinate conjunction; for example, ὅτι βλέπομεν τοὺς δούλους (because we see the slaves). The verb is sometimes implied rather than fully stated.

> **4. A relative clause** is a dependent clause beginning with a relative pronoun; for example, ὅν βλέπομεν (whom we see).

Any sentence with one main clause and at least one dependent clause is a complex sentence, regardless of the number of prepositional phrases. Any sentence with more than one main clause and at least one dependent clause is a compound-complex sentence.

> COMPLEX: εἰ ἔτι ἀνθρώποις ἤρεσκον,
> Χριστοῦ δοῦλος οὐκ ἂν ἤμην.

If I were still pleasing people, I would not be Christ's slave (Gal. 1:10).

> COMPOUND-COMPLEX: ἐξελθὼν εἶδεν πολὺν ὄχλον
> καὶ ἐσπλαγχνίσθη.

When he arrived, he saw a great crowd and had compassion (Mark 6:34).

1.2.2. Grammatical Parts of a Sentence

Many students have never learned the English grammar labels necessary for discussing the parts in a sentence. If you can use the material on phrases and clauses in the previous section (1.2.1), you can identify every part of a Greek sentence by learning only six more labels.

1.2.2.1. Subject. The subject tells who or what a sentence is about. In Greek, the subject is often not a separate word but is implied by the personal ending of the verb. The subject can be modified by adjectives, prepositional phrases, and even dependent clauses. In Greek, the subject is in the nominative case.

ἀσπάζεταί σε Ἐπαφρᾶς.

Epaphras greets you (Philem. 23).

1.2.2.2. Verb. The verb tells what action is done by or to the subject, or discusses a condition (state of being) of the subject. In Greek, verbs may be active or deponent (telling what the subject does); middle (telling what the subject both does and receives); passive (telling what is done to the subject); or without voice (telling a state of being rather than an action).

εἶπεν παραβολὴν αὐτοῖς.

He **told** them a parable (Luke 21:29).

The **predicate** is the verb and all the rest of a sentence except the subject and its modifiers; that is, the predicate is everything that is affirmed or denied about the subject. Thinking of the Greek verb alone is more helpful than thinking of an entire predicate. The verb is the single most important word in a Greek sentence.

1.2.2.3. Direct object. The direct object receives the action done by the subject. The direct object defines the limits of the action of the verb. In Greek, direct objects are usually in the accusative case. Also, few Greek passive verbs have an object. (In English, the object of a passive verb is called a retained object.) Some Greek verbs have a genitive or dative direct object.

τίς ὑμᾶς ἐβάσκανεν;

Who bewitched **you**? (Gal. 3:1).

1.2.2.4. Indirect object. Only sentences with a direct object may have an indirect object. An indirect object tells who or what receives the direct object—usually a person. Indirect objects in Greek are in the dative case. (A dative noun telling for whom the action of the verb is done in a sentence with no direct object is called a dative of advantage. An indirect object means that the sentence already has a direct object.)

εἶπεν παραβολὴν **αὐτοῖς**.

He told **them** a parable (Luke 21:29).

1.2.2.5. Subject complement. When the verb describes a condition of the subject (for example, what the subject is or becomes, how the subject feels), it often includes a word or words that complete or complement the subject. In Greek, these words are in the nominative case. There are two varieties of subject complements: (1) a predicate nominative renames the subject; (2) a predicate adjective describes the subject.

PREDICATE NOMINATIVE: ἡ ἁμαρτία ἐστὶν ἡ **ἀνομία**.

Sin is **lawlessness** (1 John 3:4).

PREDICATE ADJECTIVE: **δυνατὸς** γάρ ὁ θεός.

For God is **able** (Rom. 11:23).

1.2.2.6. Object complement. Occasionally the direct object is renamed by another accusative noun. This noun is needed to complete the sense of the direct object and is called the object complement.

Δαυὶδ οὖν **κύριον** αὐτὸν καλεῖ.

Thus David calls him **Lord** (Luke 20:44).

1.2.3. Major Constructions for a Sentence

When you understand the limited number of parts in a Greek sentence, you can appreciate that only a few patterns are possible for constructing sentences. Prepositional phrases and dependent clauses can extend a Greek sentence indefinitely, but the options for constructing basic sentences are quite limited. Every independent clause (simple sentence) falls into one of four patterns. The verb is the key to distinguishing between these four constructions.

1.2.3.1. The transitive verb pattern. In many Greek sentences verbs transfer their meaning to a direct object. Such verbs are called transitive. Context determines whether a verb is transitive or intransitive. Three varieties of this pattern appear:

SUBJECT + TRANSITIVE VERB + DIRECT OBJECT

SUBJECT + TRANSITIVE VERB + DIRECT OBJECT + INDIRECT OBJECT

SUBJECT + TRANSITIVE VERB + DIRECT OBJECT + OBJECT COMPLEMENT

The previous section gives an example of each of these (1.2.2). Of course, the subject may not be a separate word in Greek but may be implied by the personal ending of the verb. Each of the parts of the sentence may also be modified by prepositional phrases, dependent clauses, or other modifiers.

1.2.3.2. The intransitive verb pattern. An **intransitive verb** is any verb with a meaning so clear that it requires no direct object. Many verbs function either transitively or intransitively, depending on their context. Often Greek deponent verbs are exclusively intransitive.

SUBJECT + INTRANSITIVE VERB

καὶ εὐθέως **ἀνέστη**.

And immediately he **stood up** (Acts 9:34).

As with all the patterns, there may be modifiers to the subject or verb. In this example, a simple adverb modifies an intransitive verb.

1.2.3.3. The passive verb pattern. Sentences with a passive Greek verb often include a prepositional phrase expressing the (personal) agent or (impersonal) instrument doing the action. This is called an agent phrase. Thus, two varieties are possible.

SUBJECT + PASSIVE VERB

ἐβλήθη εἰς τὴν γῆν.

He was **thrown** onto the earth (Rev. 12:9).

SUBJECT + PASSIVE VERB + AGENT PHRASE

ἐβαπτίζοντο ὑπ᾽ αὐτοῦ.

They were being baptized by him (Mark 1:5).

In these examples, note the difference in function between the two prepositional phrases. In the first, the prepositional phrase is merely an adverb modifier answering the question where. In the second, an agent phrase answers the question by whom. This is more customary in a sentence with a passive verb.

1.2.3.4. The "be" verb pattern. The main Greek verbs expressing a state of being are εἰμί and γίνομαι. Verbs of being usually have a subject complement. Occasionally some other kind of modifier is used instead of a subject complement.

SUBJECT + VERB OF BEING + SUBJECT COMPLEMENT

ὁ πατήρ μου ὁ γεωργός **ἐστιν**.

My Father **is** the farmer (John 15:1).

SUBJECT + VERB OF BEING +
MODIFIER/PREPOSITIONAL PHRASE

ἐγὼ μέν **εἰμι** Παύλου.

I **am** indeed of Paul (1 Cor. 3:4).

1.3. The Paragraph

Suppose you overheard two young people talking. One said, "Wendy's is always a great place for hot potatoes." You might think of fast food. If the next sentence spoken is, "I hear that Wendy hired a great new opening act," you might remember that Wendy's is a dance club for teenagers in your town. The "hot potato" might be the latest rage in dance steps. Specific sentences can only be fully understood within a broader context.

The best preaching portion is almost always a paragraph rather than a sentence, a verse, or a word. Editions of the Greek Testament and most contemporary translations are arranged into paragraphs. You will want to learn to use the fourth edition of the United Bible Societies' *The Greek New Testament,* with its innovative Discourse Segmentation Apparatus. This carefully identifies all points at which important editions of the Greek Testament and several modern translations differ in paragraph breaks, sentence divisions, and other areas. When your Greek Testament and your preferred English Bible disagree on paragraph divisions, you must discern for yourself where the paragraph breaks ought to fall.

1.3.1. Varieties of Paragraphs

Several types of materials in the Greek New Testament appear to be paragraphs, even though they are not paragraphs in the strictest sense. Poems, for example, are divided into **stanzas** with a paragraph format (noted in the Discourse Segmentation Apparatus). You should preach from a stanza of poetry as you would preach from a paragraph of prose. See, for example, Luke 1:47–50.

The Gospels and Acts contain more narrative material than instructional (didactic) material. When you preach from a narrative passage you may prefer to use all the paragraphs of the account (see 6.2 and the related subsections). The Gospels and Acts have long been divided into standard **pericopes** or lections (selections for public reading in Christian worship services). English titles for the pericopes are labeled both in many Greek Testaments and in many English Bibles. One example is the Triumphal Entry into

Jerusalem in Luke 19:28–44. You should preach from a pericope rather than a single paragraph when your text is narrative.

From now on in this book, the word *paragraph* will also be used to designate a stanza of poetry or a pericope of narrative. In the exercises at the end of each chapter, you will study both a narrative pericope and a didactic paragraph.

1.3.2. Varieties of Sentences Within a Paragraph

Sentences in the Greek Testament are logically interdependent. Typically a paragraph has three kinds of sentences.

1. The **introductory sentence** announces the theme of a paragraph. Usually it does not have an initial coordinate conjunction. (If there is a conjunction, its purpose is to connect the paragraph with the previous paragraph.) The introductory sentence is usually but not always placed first in a paragraph.

2. The **development sentence** logically expands the introductory sentence. Usually development sentences begin with a coordinate conjunction. (When there is no such conjunction, grammarians use the term **asyndeton**, meaning "not bound.") Studying these conjunctions provides a good clue as to how the argument of a paragraph has been developed. Most development sentences exhibit one of the following logical relationships to the introductory sentence.

Cause	Result
Time	Illustration
Purpose	Explanation

3. The **summary sentence** concludes the matter of a paragraph. It is usually at or near the end of a paragraph and usually begins with a conjunction. Many paragraphs do not have summary sentences.

Chapter Summary

In intermediate Greek, students usually concentrate on sentences. They learn how to interpret clauses and phrases and they pore over the precise use of a verb tense or a noun case within a sentence. This is important and cannot be ignored.

Beyond words and sentences lie paragraphs. The most important part of this chapter is the statement, "If you want to be a credible minister of the Word, you will learn to think paragraphs." Only when you have understood an entire paragraph are you ready to begin planning to preach or teach.

Many of the chapters in this book guide you in working at the word level or the sentence level. You have missed the point of studying a Greek passage if you stop short of an entire paragraph or pericope.

Now Let's Apply!

At the end of each chapter is an opportunity to practice what we have been discussing. In each chapter we will use Matthew 4:1–11 and Philippians 1:3–11. The following exercises are meant to get you to think about words, sentences, and paragraphs. You may open an English Bible to help you with this. (In the exercises for this chapter, I have included a literalistic English translation for each sentence to ease you into the exercises.) The first sentence for each Greek Testament selection has been completed as an example. An answer key is located in the back of the book, but spend at least half an hour working on the exercise before you look for the answers.

1. Underline all verb forms.

2. Find and label several of each of the following: subject, direct object, indirect object, and subject complement.

3. Underline whether the sentence is simple, compound, complex, or compound-complex. At the end of every Greek sentence is the following code: SIM CPND CPLX C-C.

4. Above at least five verbs that you underlined, note which one of the following four patterns is used: T = transitive; I = intransitive; P = passive; B = verb of being.

Matthew 4

^{1}τότε ὁ Ἰησοῦς (subject) <u>ἀνήχθη</u> (P) εἰς τὴν ἔρημον ὑπὸ τοῦ πνεύματος, <u>πειρασθῆναι</u> (P) ὑπὸ τοῦ διαβόλου. ^{1}Then Jesus was led into the desert by the Spirit, to be tempted by the devil. SIM CPND <u>CPLX</u> C-C

²καὶ νηστεύσας ἡμέρας τεσσεράκοντα καὶ νύκτας τεσσεράκοντα ὕστερον ἐπείνασεν. ²And having fasted forty days and forty nights afterward he hungered. SIM CPND CPLX C-C

³καὶ προσελθὼν ὁ πειράζων εἶπεν αὐτῷ, εἰ υἱὸς εἶ τοῦ θεοῦ, εἰπὲ ἵνα οἱ λίθοι οὗτοι ἄρτοι γένωνται. ³And the tempter coming to him said to him, "If you are the Son of God, command that these stones become loaves." SIM CPND CPLX C-C

⁴ὁ δὲ ἀποκριθεὶς εἶπεν, γέγραπται, οὐκ ἐπ᾽ ἄρτῳ μόνῳ ζήσεται ὁ ἄνθρωπος, ἀλλ᾽ ἐπὶ παντὶ ῥήματι ἐκπορευομένῳ διὰ στόματος θεοῦ. ⁴But he answering said, "It is written, 'Not by bread only shall man live but by every word proceeding from the mouth of God.'" SIM CPND CPLX C-C

⁵τότε παραλαμβάνει αὐτὸν ὁ διάβολος εἰς τὴν ἁγίαν πόλιν, καὶ ἔστησεν αὐτὸν ἐπὶ τὸ πτερύγιον τοῦ ἱεροῦ, ⁶καὶ λέγει αὐτῷ, εἰ υἱὸς εἶ τοῦ θεοῦ, βάλε σεαυτὸν κάτω· γέγραπται γὰρ ὅτι τοῖς ἀγγέλοις αὐτοῦ ἐντελεῖται περὶ σοῦ καὶ ἐπὶ χειρῶν ἀροῦσίν σε, μήποτε προσκόψῃς πρὸς λίθον τὸν πόδα σου. ⁵Then the devil takes him into the holy city, and he stood him upon the pinnacle of the temple, ⁶and he says to him, "If you are the Son of God, throw yourself down, for it is written, 'To his angels he will command concerning you, and on their hands they will carry you, lest you strike against a stone your foot.'" SIM CPND CPLX C-C

⁷ἔφη αὐτῷ ὁ Ἰησοῦ, πάλιν γέγραπται, οὐκ ἐκπειράσεις κύριον τὸν θεόν σου. ⁷Jesus said to him, "Again it is written, 'You shall not test the Lord your God.'" SIM CPND CPLX C-C

⁸πάλιν παραλαμβάνει αὐτὸν ὁ διάβολος εἰς ὄρος ὑψηλὸν λίαν, καὶ δείκνυσιν αὐτῷ πάσας τὰς βασιλείας τοῦ κόσμου καὶ τὴν δόξαν αὐτῶν, ⁹καὶ εἶπεν αὐτῷ, ταῦτά σοι πάντα δώσω ἐὰν πεσὼν προσκυνήσῃς μοι. ⁸Again the devil takes him unto a very high mountain, and he shows to him all the kingdoms of the world and their glory, ⁹and he said to him, "All these things to you I will give if falling you worship me." SIM CPND CPLX C-C

¹⁰τότε λέγει αὐτῷ ὁ Ἰησοῦ, ὕπαγε, Σατανᾶ· γέγραπται γάρ, κύριον τὸν θεόν σου προσκυνήσεις καὶ αὐτῷ μόνῳ λατρεύσεις. ¹⁰Then Jesus says to him, "Depart, Satan, for it is written, 'You shall worship the Lord your God and you shall serve him only.'" SIM CPND CPLX C-C

¹¹τότε ἀφίησιν αὐτὸν ὁ διάβολος, καὶ ἰδοὺ ἄγγελοι προσῆλθον καὶ διηκόνουν αὐτῷ. ¹¹Then the devil leaves him, and behold angels came and served him. SIM CPND CPLX C-C

Philippians 1

³εὐχαριστῶ (T) τῷ θεῷ (direct object) μου ἐπὶ πάσῃ τῇ μνείᾳ ὑμῶν, ⁴πάντοτε ἐν πάσῃ δεήσει μου ὑπὲρ πάντων ὑμῶν μετὰ χαρᾶς τὴν δέησιν (direct object) ποιούμενος (T), ⁵ἐπὶ τῇ κοιν-ωνίᾳ ὑμῶν εἰς τὸ εὐαγγέλιον ἀπὸ τῆς πρώτης ἡμέρας ἄχρι τοῦ νῦν, ⁶πεποιθὼς (T) αὐτὸ τοῦτο (direct object), ὅτι ὁ ἐναρξά-μενος (subject, T) ἐν ὑμῖν ἔργον ἀγαθὸν ἐπιτελέσει ἄχρι

ἡμέρας Χριστοῦ Ἰησοῦ· ⁷καθώς <u>ἐστιν</u> (B) δίκαιον ἐμοὶ τοῦτο <u>φρονεῖν</u> (T) ὑπὲρ πάντων ὑμῶν, διὰ τὸ <u>ἔχειν</u> με ἐν τῇ καρδίᾳ ὑμᾶς, ἔν τε τοῖς δεσμοῖς μου καὶ ἐν τῇ ἀπολογίᾳ καὶ βεβαιώσει τοῦ εὐαγγελίου συγκοινωνούς μου τῆς χάριτος πάντας ὑμᾶς <u>ὄντας</u> (B). ³I thank my God upon every remembrance of you, ⁴always in my every prayer for you all with joy making the prayer, ⁵for your fellowship in the gospel from the first day until now, ⁶persuaded of this thing, that the one who began in you a good work will complete it until the day of Christ Jesus; ⁷even as it is right for me to think this about you all, because I have you in (my) heart, both in my bonds and in the defense and confirmation of the gospel you all being partakers with me of grace. SIM CPND <u>CPLX</u> C-C

⁸μάρτυς γάρ μου ὁ θεός, ὡς ἐπιποθῶ πάντας ὑμᾶς ἐν σπλάγχνοις Χριστοῦ Ἰησοῦ. ⁸For God is my witness, how I long for you all with the inward parts of Christ Jesus. SIM CPND CPLX C-C

⁹καὶ τοῦτο προσεύχομαι, ἵνα ἡ ἀγάπη ὑμῶν ἔτι μᾶλλον καὶ μᾶλλον περισσεύῃ ἐν ἐπιγνώσει καὶ πάσῃ αἰσθήσει, ¹⁰εἰς τὸ δοκιμάζειν ὑμᾶς τὰ διαφέροντα, ἵνα ἦτε εἰλικρινεῖς καὶ ἀπρόσκοποι εἰς ἡμέραν Χριστοῦ, ¹¹πεπληρωμένοι καρπὸν δικαιοσύνης τὸν διὰ Ἰησοῦ Χριστοῦ εἰς δόξαν καὶ ἔπαινον θεοῦ. ⁹And this I pray, that your love yet more and more may abound in knowledge and all insight, ¹⁰in order that you may approve the things which differ, so that you may be pure and blameless unto the day of Christ, ¹¹filled with the fruit of righteousness which (is) through Jesus Christ unto the glory and praise of God. SIM CPND CPLX C-C

2 | The Greek Paragraph

$\mathbf{W}$e have now reviewed the basic structure of Greek. In this chapter we focus on the overall sense of an individual Greek paragraph. Many preachers begin and end with word studies, but you are learning to think paragraphs.

Suppose you are planning a sermon or Bible study. You choose a paragraph of text. You read the text in English several times. You even pick your way through the Greek text. Now you are ready to start your detailed study. The best way to understand your paragraph is to develop a **paragraph flow**.

Before coming to terms with exegetical details, you must have a general sense of an author's flow of thought within the paragraph. The author left you clues by the way he joined clauses. What a writer subordinates in **syntax** is usually subordinate in his thinking. (Syntax refers to the way words are arranged or organized within a sentence. Grammar is a broader term that includes the proper formation of individual words.)

2.1. Purpose of a Paragraph Flow

Some readers remember painful experiences with traditional diagramming techniques in their English grammar classes. This method had a grammatical position for every word. The sentence, "John's big brother clearly saw apples in the tree," was diagrammed like this:

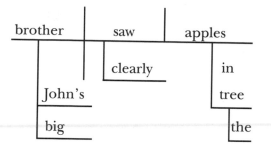

This system forced students to consider the syntactical placement of each word individually. This method is time consuming and rarely taught in English grammar classes anymore. Greek students usually find it overwhelming. Most syntactical relationships within a Greek sentence are fairly obvious. One further weakness of this approach is that such detailed diagrams almost always stopped at the sentence level.

In contrast to this traditional method, our method examines the thought flow of a paragraph. Our objective is to uncover the overall structure of a Greek paragraph, in preparation for in-depth study of words, phrases, and clauses.

2.2. Identifying the Elements of a Paragraph Flow

Begin your work by photocopying the selected paragraph from your Greek New Testament. On this copy you will identify three elements of a paragraph flow: sentence types, verb forms, and structure markers.

2.2.1. Identifying Sentence Types

In section 1.3.2. we discussed three sentence types: the **introductory sentence,** the **development sentence**, and the **summary sentence**. The easiest way to categorize sentences is to reread your paragraph in English, searching for the logical relationship of each sentence to the paragraph as a whole. Then turn to your Greek text. Above each Greek period and colon (printed as a raised dot), write I, D, or S to note what sentence type precedes the period or colon. After finishing detailed exegetical study, you may change your mind about a particular sentence, but now you are at least starting to establish relationships among sentences.

2.2.2. Identifying Verb Forms

Because verbs are the most important parts of Greek sentences, begin your paragraph flow by underlining all verbs. Include all verbs and verbal elements—main verbs, dependent verbs, participles, and infinitives. Since the action in written human communication is expressed with verbs, verbs often provide the ultimate direction for your sermons.

2.2.3. Identifying Structure Markers

Structure markers are relational words. They tell how a speaker or writer's thoughts are related. Although this term may be new to you, you are already familiar with structural markers. In Greek there are four kinds of structural markers to look for. Draw a vertical line to the left of each one that you find.

2.2.3.1. Prepositions. Most prepositions connect a noun or pronoun to the rest of a sentence in a prepositional phrase. The following is a list of the **formal prepositions:**

ἀνά	διά	ἐπί	παρά	σύν
ἀντί	εἰς	κατά	περί	ὑπέρ
ἀπό	ἐκ (ἐξ)	μετά	πρό	ὑπό
	ἐν		προς	

Some prepositions are contracted with an apostrophe when the following word begins with a vowel.

In addition to the formal prepositions, some Greek words sometimes function as prepositions. These are called **functional prepositions,** though most are technically classified as adverbs. The following words can function as prepositions:

ἄχρι	ἕνεκεν	ἐπάνω	ὀπίσω
ἐγγύς	ἐνώπιον	ἕως	πέραν
ἔμπροσθεν	ἔξω	μέχρι	χωρίς

2.2.3.2. Relative pronouns. Relative pronouns are one way to connect a dependent clause to a sentence. You will find only two lexical entries for relative pronouns in your dictionary, but each has several spellings (syntactical words), depending on case, gender, and number: ὅς, ἥ, ὅ (who, which, that) and ὅστις, ἥτις, ὅτι (whoever, whichever). Place a vertical line in front of each relative pronoun, just as you did before each preposition. (Some grammarians also include the relative adverbs ὅτε, οὗ, and ὡς. I have chosen to include them with the subordinate conjunctions below.)

2.2.3.3. Coordinate conjunctions. The **coordinate conjunction** is a word that joins sentences, verbs, or other grammatical equals within a sentence. Write a vertical line before all coordinate conjunctions that join clauses; do not mark coordinate conjunctions that merely connect words or prepositional phrases. Coordinate conjunctions show several logical relationships. The following list shows the most important coordinate conjunctions. The translations are suggestive. These categories often overlap.

Continuation	καί, δέ, τε (and)
Disjunction	ἤ, εἴτε (or)
Negative	οὐδέ, οὔτε, μηδέ, μήτε (and not, not)
Inference	οὖν, δίο, ἄρα (therefore)
Cause	γάρ (for, because)
Adversative	ἀλλά, δέ, μὲν . . . δέ (but) πλήν, μέντοι, καίτοι (however)

2.2.3.4. Subordinate conjunctions. These are words that link a dependent clause to a main clause. Please mark each subordinate conjunction with a vertical line. A number of relationships are possible with the subordinate conjunctions. The most important are listed below. The translations suggested are not absolute, as any lexicon indicates.

Purpose	ἵνα, ὅπως (in order that)
Result	ὥστε, ἵνα (so that)
Cause	ὅτι, διότι, ἐπεί (because)
Condition	εἰ, ἐάν, εἴπερ (if)
Concession	εἰ καί, ἐὰν καί, κἄν (even if)
Comparison	καθώς, ὥσπερ, ὡς (just as)

Place	ὅπου, οὗ (where)
Time	ὅτε, ὅταν, ὡς, ὡς ἄν (when) ἕως (until)
Statement	ὅτι (that, ". . ." = content of what is known, felt, seen, etc., or as a marker of direct or indirect speech)

Chapter 6 expands and develops many of these concepts.

2.2.4. Identifying the Elements of Paragraph Flow in James 1:2–8

Once you become adept at doing this, you can mark any Greek paragraph in less than ten minutes. I have given an example of how this preliminary step looks by using the paragraph of James 1:2-8. I have added some extra indentions to make it easier for you to follow, but this is really only one paragraph. Before studying this example, open your English Bible and read through the paragraph two or three times. Feel free to consult your English translation as well as any other Greek helps you wish. Do not feel that you must understand every word.

²πᾶσαν χαρὰν <u>ἡγήσασθε</u>, ἀδελφοί μου, | ὅταν πειρασμοῖς <u>περιπέσητε</u> ποικίλοις, ³ <u>γινώσκοντες</u> | ὅτι τὸ δοκίμιον ὑμῶν τῆς πίστεως <u>κατεργάζεται</u> ὑπομονήν· (I)

⁴ἡ | δὲ ὑπομονὴ ἔργον τέλειον <u>ἐχέτω</u>, | ἵνα <u>ἦτε</u> τέλειοι καὶ ὁλόκληροι, | ἐν μηδενὶ <u>λειπόμενοι</u>. (D)

⁵ | εἰ | δέ τις ὑμῶν <u>λείπεται</u> σοφίας, <u>αἰτείτω</u> | παρὰ τοῦ <u>διδόντος</u> θεοῦ πᾶσιν ἁπλῶς | καὶ μὴ <u>ὀνειδίζοντος</u> | καὶ <u>δοθήσεται</u> αὐτῷ. (D)

⁶<u>αἰτείτω</u> | δέ | ἐν πίστει, μηδὲν <u>διακρινόμενος</u>, ὁ | γὰρ <u>διακρινόμενος</u> <u>ἔοικεν</u> κλύδωνι θαλάσσης <u>ἀνεμιζομένῳ</u> | καὶ <u>ῥιπιζομένῳ</u>· (D)

⁷μὴ | γὰρ <u>οἰέσθω</u> ὁ ἄνθρωπος ἐκεῖνος | ὅτι <u>λήμψεταί</u> τι | παρὰ τοῦ κυρίου, ⁸ἀνὴρ δίψυχος, ἀκατάστατος | ἐν πάσαις ταῖς ὁδοῖς αὐτοῦ. (D)

What have we accomplished so far? We have discovered that James has a main point, as noted in his introductory sentence: believers must rejoice at trials because of the wonderful outcome. This outcome is explained and illustrated in the four development sentences. There is no summary sentence. James uses many verbs, which should be explored later. He also loads his writing with structure markers. There are no relative pronouns in this example, but several prepositions, coordinate conjunctions, and subordinate conjunctions. These help us trace his thinking, as will become evident as our paragraph flow develops.

2.3. Procedures for a Paragraph Flow

After you have discovered the syntactical "joints" the author used, it is relatively easy to divide his writing into clauses. Then you can readily identify other aspects of the paragraph. Although this procedure seems mechanical at first, once you get the hang of it, it will become easier. My students learned that this is easy after a little practice.

2.3.1. Copying the Clauses

Remember that there are only two kinds of clauses by form: **main clauses** (1.2.1.1) and **dependent clauses** (1.2.1.3). Main clauses usually have an indicative or imperative verb. Dependent clauses often have a subjunctive verb, participle, or infinitive, but they always have one of these: a relative pronoun, a subordinate conjunction, a participle, or an infinitive. In your preliminaries you already marked these, so they should not be hard to figure out.

Place the Greek text that you have marked in front of you on your desk. Beside this, place a separate sheet of double-spaced ruled paper. Using a pencil (not a pen), copy each clause from the Greek paragraph on a separate line on the ruled sheet.

Line up all main clauses at the left margin. If a clause is too long to fit on one line, continue it on to the next line, indented about two or three spaces. I use an arrow (→) at the end of the line as a reminder that the same clause continues on the next line down.

Indent every dependent clause one inch. When you have finished doing this, you will end up with a series of Greek clauses on your page: the first set at the left margin; the second set indented an inch. Keep to the Greek word order as much as possible. When a dependent clause is embedded (or nested) within another clause, give it a separate line, but indicate its original place by ellipsis dots (...). In most instances, a dependent clause "depends on" (modifies) the clause above it (or the closest independent clause above it) in your paragraph flow. When a clause depends on a clause that follows it, note this with a down arrow (↓) in front of the clause.

2.3.2. Marking the Verb Forms

Transfer this information from your marked Greek text to your paragraph flow page. This is how I recommend noting verb forms.

1. Double underline the verbs of main clauses (clauses beginning at the left margin). These verbs require more attention than others. Often you can build your message simply by following these in sequence.

2. Single underline all the other verb forms. This includes all the verbs of the dependent clauses. I suggest that you also underline all other verb forms as well, such as participles functioning as simple adjective modifiers. These underlined verbs may become a fruitful source of sermon subpoints.

2.3.3. Marking the Structure Markers

You marked these in your preliminary work by putting vertical lines to the left of all prepositions, relative pronouns, subordinate conjunctions and coordinate conjunctions that join clauses. Here is how these are handled on your paragraph flow page.

1. Capitalize or circle all the structure markers. (At first, circling them may be easier. I always capitalize, since the page looks less cluttered.) Having these in your paragraph flow alerts you to possible parallels, contrasts, or other sequences that merit further study.

2. Put braces around all prepositional phrases. (You should have capitalized or circled the prepositions already.) Although prepositional phrases seem minor, they can carry quite important theological information. Marking prepositional phrases at this point makes you aware of such possibilities at an early stage.

3. Note the form of each clause in the right margin. For main clauses, note whether the clause belongs to an **introductory sentence** (INT), **development sentence** (DEV), or **summary sentence** (SUM). For dependent clauses, note usage of a **subordinate conjunction** (SUB), **relative pronoun** (REL), **participle** (PAR), or **infinitive** (INF). Think about how the author communicated meaning in the paragraph.

2.3.4. Preliminary Marking of Clause Functions

You are not ready yet to make final decisions about the exact exegetical relationship of clauses to each other. This comes only after you have studied the verbs more extensively. You can begin thinking about how the information of the paragraph is logically related. A dependent clause functions in only three basic ways: as an **adjective** (describing some noun or pronoun); as a **substantive** (standing for a noun); or as an **adverb**. Adverb relationships are the most helpful for sermon purposes. The data about subordinate conjunctions earlier in this chapter (2.2.3.4) comes into play in thinking about adverb relationships. In noting your preliminary decisions about clause function, put the information at the right margin just to the right of your form notations. I separate the two with a slash.

2.3.5. Procedure Applied to James 1:2–8

Your paragraph flow may not look as polished as the following example. Remember that you are to use a pencil so that you can correct yourself. Don't get bogged down. You will gain speed. If you have done your preliminary marking on a photocopied sheet, it should be able to lay out a paragraph flow in half an hour—once you've had a little practice.

Paragraph Flow of James 2:1–8	
²πᾶσαν χαρὰν <u>ἡγήσασθε</u>, ἀδελφοί μου,	INT
ΟΤΑΝ πειρασμοῖς <u>περιπέσητε</u> ➜ ποικίλοις,	SUB/time
³<u>γινώσκοντες</u>	PAR/cause
ΟΤΙ τὸ δοκίμιον ὑμῶν τῆς πίστεως ➜ <u>κατεργάζεται</u> ὑπομονήν·	SUB/statement
⁴ἡ ΔΕ ὑπομονὴ ἔργον τέλειον <u>ἐχέτω</u>,	DEV/continuation
ΙΝΑ <u>ἦτε</u> τέλειοι καὶ ὁλόκληροι,	SUB /purpose
{ΕΝ μηδενὶ} <u>λειπόμενοι</u>.	PAR/result
↓ ⁵ΕΙ ΔΕ τις ὑμῶν <u>λείπεται</u> σοφίας,	SUB/condition
<u>αἰτείτω</u> {ΠΑΡΑ τοῦ . . . θεοῦ}	DEV/continuation
<u>διδόντος</u> . . . πᾶσιν ἁπλῶς	PAR/adjective
ΚΑΙ μὴ <u>ὀνειδίζοντος</u>,	PAR/adjective
ΚΑΙ <u>δοθήσεται</u> αὐτῷ.	DEV/continuation
⁶<u>αἰτείτω</u> ΔΕ {ΕΝ πίστει},	DEV/adversative
' μηδὲν <u>διακρινόμενος</u>,	PAR/manner
ὁ ΓΑΡ <u>διακρινόμενος</u> <u>ἔοικεν</u> κλύδωνι ➜ θαλάσσης <u>ἀνεμιζομένῳ</u> καὶ <u>ῥιπιζομένῳ</u>·	DEV/cause
⁷μὴ ΓΑΡ <u>οἰέσθω</u> ὁ ἄνθρωπος ἐκεῖνος	DEV/cause
ΟΤΙ <u>λήμψεταί</u> τι {ΠΑΡΑ τοῦ κυρίου},➜ ⁸ἀνὴρ δίψυχος, ἀκατάστατος ➜ {ΕΝ πάσαις ταῖς ὁδοῖς αὐτοῦ}.	SUB/statement

2.4. Patterns Within a Paragraph Flow

As you study a paragraph flow, you will recognize several patterns. Take a highlighter or colored pen and connect any of the following elements.

2.4.1. Repeated Vocabulary

What an author repeats was important to him. In the James sample, two verb forms are repeated exactly: *let him ask* and *not doubt-*

ing. Two nouns are repeated with only case variations: *faith* and *patience*. The adjective *mature* occurs twice. One prepositional phrase occurs twice (with a slight variation): *from God* and *from the Lord*. Noting these now can remind you of items that need attention in your later study.

2.4.2. Negative and Positive

Look for negative statements, balanced by positives. Watch for any negative word—those beginning with ἀ- or οὐ- or μη-. These provide clues to meaning that are effective when developed in a sermon. In James 1 notice the following:

- Results of the working of patience (v. 4): negatively, "not lacking anything;" positively, "mature and complete."
- God's giving to all (v. 5): negatively, "not finding fault;" positively, "generous."
- How to ask (v. 6): negatively, "not doubting;" positively, "in faith."
- In verse 7, the negative precedes an example for all people to avoid. Verses 2–6a are the positive statements.

2.4.3. Comparison or Contrast

Negatives are one kind of contrast, but there are many others. Several contrasts occur in the James 1 paragraph: asking and receiving; mature (v. 4) and doubleminded (v. 8). One comparison stands out: James's illustration of the doubter to a wind-tossed wave.

2.5. Making a Paragraph Flow Summary

Because we have been using James 1:2–8 as a model for developing a paragraph flow, we will use it to show how a paragraph flow summary could look. There is no one right way to do this. The point of the summary is to commit yourself in writing so that you can see where you need to devote further attention.

1. **Write a summary sentence.** Summarize the paragraph in a single English sentence such as the following: "Christians must welcome trials because these help develop complete maturity, which stands in sharp contrast to the doubts of the unstable ones."

2. **Identify the important verbs.** List the verbs that seem most important. Note five or six that seem to merit closer attention in a vertical column. Beside each one, note your preliminary understanding of the verb. You might want to jot down how this might

be used in a sermon (for example, "command for today; result; narrative value only").

ἡγήσασθε (count it)—main command of introductory sentence
γινώσκοντες (knowing)—believers are to know what follows
αἰτείτω (let him ask)—twice; present tense; command
διακρινόμενος (doubting)—twice; strong negative word
λήμψεταί (he will receive)—the flip side of "giving" (v. 5); related to "asking"; see Sermon on Mount—"ask, seek, knock"

3.   List important structure markers. List five or six structure markers (prepositions, relative pronouns, or conjunctions) that appear to be prominent in showing the author's flow of thinking. Again, put them in a vertical list and note your preliminary understanding as well as sermon potential.

ὅτι—v. 3 = statement of what Christians are to know
ἵνα—v. 4 = purpose of testing is patience; purpose of patience is maturity; logical sequence is important here
εἰ—v. 5 = assumed true? Does James imply that this is frequent?
ἐν—v. 6 = "in faith." Does this = "with faith"? Study!
γάρ—v. 7 = an important reason to avoid doubt is given.

4.   List important patterns. List five or six patterns you found within the paragraph marked from the guidelines in section 2.4. Again, compile these in a vertical column so that you can get your observations in writing. Examine the following examples from James:

τέλειος—repetition; importance of maturity. Study this word!
ask/give/receive—This pattern of relationships is in focus here.
doubt vs. faith—Strong contrast; note that Christians are addressed.
mature/complete vs. doublemined/unstable—strong contrast.
wind-tossed wave—effective sermon opener? Look in my files for ocean stories.

5. Preliminary application/relevance. Conclude with a statement that tells what you think the value of your paragraph is for application to today's Christians. Of course, your further study will modify this, but even at this stage you need to consider the relevance of the paragraph for living. The following paragraph is an example:

"Christians can be joyful by focusing on what God wants to accomplish through their problems: spiritual maturity. They are to keep asking God in faith for the wisdom they need to make it through trials. God has promised to answer yes to such requests, but He answers no to doubters. The role of faith in the face of difficulties is the most important current application of this text."

How to Develop a Paragraph Flow

I. Do the Preliminaries

1. Determine the sentence types   = Intro., **Dev.**, **S**um.

2. Find all verb forms   = <u>underline</u>

3. Identify structure markers   = I vertical mark

   (See chart on next page)

II. Write Out the Paragraph Flow

1. Give each clause a line—if main, at left; if dependent, indent.

2. Mark the verbs = <u>verbs of main clauses</u>; <u>all others</u>

3. Note structure markers
    = capitalize: PREPOSITION/RELATIVES/CONJUNCTIONS
    = braces: {prepositional phrases}

4. Note the form of each clause in right margin

MAIN	DEPENDENT
INTroductory	RELative
DEVelopment	PARticiple
SUMmary	INFinitive
	SUBordinate conjunction

5. Note function of each clause in right margin: adjective, substantive, adverb (if main clause, use initial coordinate conjunction for clue) (if adverb function, be more specific, for example, "result")

III. Discover Any Patterns in the Paragraph

1. Repition

2. Negative and positive

3. Comparison and contrast

FORMAL PREPOSITIONS		FUNCTIONAL PREPOSITIONS		COORDINATE CONJUNCTIONS		SUBORDINATE CONJUNCTIONS	
ἀνά	μετά	ἄχρι	ἐπάνω	μὲν … δέ	ἄρα	διότι	ὅπως
ἀντί	παρά	ἐγγύς	ἕως	μέντοι	ἀλλά	ἐάν (καί)	ὅταν
ἀπό	περί	ἔμπροσθεν	μέχρι	μηδέ	γάρ	εἰ (καί)	ὅτε
διά	πρό	ἕνεκεν	ὀπίσω	μήτε	δέ	εἴπερ	ὅτι
εἰς	πρός	ἐνώπιον	πέραν	οὐδέ	διό	ἕως	οὗ
ἐκ (ἐξ)	σύν	ἔξω	χωρίς	οὖν	εἴτε	ἵνα	ὡς (ἄν)
ἐν	ὑπέρ	**RELATIVES**		οὔτε	ἤ	κἄν	ὥσπερ
ἐπί	ὑπό	ὅς, ἥ, ὅ		πλήν	καί	καθώς	ὥστε
κατά		ὅστις, ἥτις		τε	καίτοι	ὅπου	

IV. Summarize the Paragraph Flow

1. Summarize the paragraph in a single sentence.

2. List 5–6 important verbs vertically and notate.

3. List 5–6 important structure markers and notate.

4. List 5–6 important patterns and notate.

5. State in a preliminary way the application value of the paragraph for today.

For Further Reading

Fee, Gordon. *New Testament Exegesis: A Handbook for Students and Pastors,* 60–77. Philadelphia: Westminster Press, 1983.

Kaiser, Walter C., Jr. *Toward an Exegetical Theology: Biblical Exegesis for Preaching and Teaching,* 95–104, 165–81. Grand Rapids: Baker Book House, 1981.

MacDonald, William G. *Greek Enchiridion: A Concise Handbook of Grammar for Translation and Exegesis,* 139–52. Peabody, Mass.: Hendrickson Publishers, 1986.

Osborne, Grant R. *The Hermeneutical Spiral: A Comprehensive Introduction to Biblical Interpretation,* 27–40. Downers Grove, Ill.: Inter-Varsity Press, 1991.

Now Let's Apply!

The text of Matthew 4:1–11 and Philippians 1:3–11 is reproduced below. Follow the guidelines of this chapter and develop a paragraph flow for each text. Use your English Bible if you need to. An answer key is located in the back of the book.

1. Do the preliminaries, using the text printed here (see 2.2.1–3).

2. Using a pencil, develop paragraph flows for each text, using your own paper (see 2.3.1–4).

3. Use a highlighter or colored pens to mark any patterns you discover (see 2.4.1–3).

4. Summarize the paragraph flow, using your own paper (see 2.4.4).

5. Each set of verses below is printed as a single paragraph. This will force you to examine relationships between sen-

tences without any visual clues. For the Matthew passage you will note several introductions to speech and to Scripture quotations. You may want to treat all such introductions as well as all quoted material as separate development "sentences," even though they are syntactically enclosed within a longer sentence.

Matthew 4

¹τότε ὁ Ἰησοῦς ἀνήχθη εἰς τὴν ἔρημον ὑπὸ τοῦ πνεύματος, πειρασθῆναι ὑπὸ τοῦ διαβόλου. ²καὶ νηστεύσας ἡμέρας τεσσεράκοντα καὶ νύκτας τεσσεράκοντα ὕστερον ἐπείνασεν. ³καὶ προσελθὼν ὁ πειράζων εἶπεν αὐτῷ, εἰ υἱὸς εἶ τοῦ θεοῦ, εἰπὲ ἵνα οἱ λίθοι οὗτοι ἄρτοι γένωνται. ⁴ὁ δὲ ἀποκριθεὶς εἶπεν, γέγραπται, οὐκ ἐπ᾽ ἄρτῳ μόνῳ ζήσεται ὁ ἄνθρωπος, ἀλλ᾽ ἐπὶ παντὶ ῥήματι ἐκπορευομένῳ διὰ στόματος θεοῦ. ⁵τότε παραλαμβάνει αὐτὸν ὁ διάβολος εἰς τὴν ἁγίαν πόλιν, καὶ ἔστησεν αὐτὸν ἐπὶ τὸ πτερύγιον τοῦ ἱεροῦ, ⁶καὶ λέγει αὐτῷ, εἰ υἱὸς εἶ τοῦ θεοῦ, βάλε σεαυτὸν κάτω· γέγραπται γὰρ ὅτι τοῖς ἀγγέλοις αὐτοῦ ἐντελεῖται περὶ σοῦ καὶ ἐπὶ χειρῶν ἀροῦσίν σε, μήποτε προσκόψῃς πρὸς λίθον τὸν πόδα σου. ⁷ἔφη αὐτῷ ὁ Ἰησοῦς, πάλιν γέγραπται, οὐκ ἐκπειράσεις κύριον τὸν θεόν σου. ⁸πάλιν παραλαμβάνει αὐτὸν ὁ διάβολος εἰς ὄρος ὑψηλὸν λίαν, καὶ δείκνυσιν αὐτῷ πάσας τὰς βασιλείας τοῦ κόσμου καὶ τὴν δόξαν αὐτῶν, ⁹καὶ εἶπεν αὐτῷ, ταῦτά σοι πάντα δώσω ἐὰν πεσὼν προσκυνήσῃς μοι. ¹⁰τότε λέγει αὐτῷ ὁ Ἰησοῦς, ὕπαγε, Σατανᾶ· γέγραπται γάρ, κύριον τὸν θεόν σου προσκυνήσεις καὶ αὐτῷ μόνῳ λατρεύσεις. ¹¹τότε ἀφίησιν αὐτὸν ὁ διάβολος, καὶ ἰδοὺ ἄγγελοι προσῆλθον καὶ διηκόνουν αὐτῷ.

Philippians 1

³εὐχαριστῶ τῷ θεῷ μου ἐπὶ πάσῃ τῇ μνείᾳ ὑμῶν, ⁴πάντοτε ἐν πάσῃ δεήσει μου ὑπὲρ πάντων ὑμῶν μετὰ χαρᾶς τὴν δέησιν ποιούμενος, ⁵ἐπὶ τῇ κοινωνίᾳ ὑμῶν εἰς τὸ εὐαγγέλιον ἀπὸ τῆς πρώτης ἡμέρας ἄχρι τοῦ νῦν, ⁶πεποιθὼς αὐτὸ τοῦτο, ὅτι ὁ ἐναρξάμενος ἐν ὑμῖν ἔργον ἀγαθὸν ἐπιτελέσει ἄχρι ἡμέρας Χριστοῦ Ἰησοῦ ⁷καθώς ἐστιν δίκαιον ἐμοὶ τοῦτο φρονεῖν ὑπὲρ πάντων ὑμῶν, διὰ τὸ ἔχειν με ἐν τῇ καρδίᾳ ὑμᾶς, ἔν τε τοῖς δεσμοῖς μου καὶ ἐν τῇ ἀπολογίᾳ καὶ βεβαιώσει τοῦ εὐαγγελίου συγκοινωνούς μου τῆς χάριτος πάντας ὑμᾶς ὄντας. ⁸μάρτυς γάρ μου ὁ θεός, ὡς ἐπιποθῶ πάντας ὑμᾶς ἐν σπλάγχνοις Χριστοῦ Ἰησοῦ. ⁹καὶ τοῦτο προσεύχομαι, ἵνα ἡ ἀγάπη ὑμῶν ἔτι μᾶλλον καὶ μᾶλλον περισσεύῃ ἐν ἐπιγνώσει καὶ πάσῃ αἰσθήσει, ¹⁰εἰς τὸ δοκιμάζειν ὑμᾶς τὰ διαφέροντα, ἵνα ἦτε εἰλικρινεῖς καὶ ἀπρόσκοποι εἰς ἡμέραν Χριστοῦ, ¹¹πεπληρωμένοι καρπὸν δικαιοσύνης τὸν διὰ Ἰησοῦ Χριστοῦ εἰς δόξαν καὶ ἔπαινον θεοῦ.

3

The Sense
of Greek Tense

One of the first lessons Greek students learn is that the Greek tense works quite differently than the English tense. You probably learned that tense in Greek represents *kind of action* more than *time of action*. This is true, but remember that English tenses tell kind of action too. Consider the following English present tense forms.

Simple	he builds
Emphatic	he does build
Progressive	he is building
Iterative	he keeps building

There are slight but real differences in meaning among these four constructions. Few of us were taught them in English grammar class, yet we use them intuitively. Similarly, Paul and the other New Testament writers did not think consciously about whether a particular verb was **literary aorist** or **gnomic future**. They used the language naturally and correctly.

Our task in approaching tense as a factor in preaching is to understand what the biblical authors assumed automatically. Sometimes we find no special meaning at all. Consider these two statements: "Joe builds houses for a living" and "Joe keeps building houses for a living." What is the difference between them? Not much. We must not read more into tense than is there.

Most Greek tenses were used with ordinary meanings that are not particularly significant. As with English, however, each **tense** could be used in a specialized way. Consider the following sentence: "I am going to Japan in two weeks." Here the present tense refers to future time. The ordinary sense of a particular tense will usually be found in a given instance, but a special sense is possible when context draws it to our attention.

For the pastor or Bible teacher, three Greek tenses are primary: the **aorist tense**, the **present tense**, and the **perfect tense**. These three are by far the most frequently used tenses in the Greek Testament. These same three tenses are widely found both inside and outside the **indicative mood**. The indicative is the normal mood for ordinary speech and writing and indicates that the action of the verb is actual rather than potential. The indicative refers to real action; other moods refer to potential action. Non-indicative Greek verbs are one of the following: **subjunctive mood**, **imperative mood**, **optative mood**, **infinitive**, or **participle**.

3.1. Aorist

The aorist is the workhorse tense. It is more frequently used in both indicative and non-indicative forms than is any other tense. Greek routinely uses the aorist unless there is some particular reason to use another tense. The aorist has no meaning in and of itself—no matter what you have heard to the contrary.

To understand the aorist tense, think of an action confined to a small circle. An aorist tense form says nothing at all about whether the action was completed or terminated, nor is anything included about the beginning or the process of an action. An aorist verb form merely looks at the action as a whole. Sometimes this is called simple or unspecified action.

What about the frequently stated idea that aorist verbs are punctiliar or point-of-time or once-for-all? This idea does not stand up. Consider this example.

ἐπορεύθη ο Ἰησοῦς τοῖς σάββασιν διὰ τῶν σπορίμων.

Jesus **went through** the grainfields on the Sabbath (Matt. 12:1).

The action took up an extended period of time; in fact, the other Gospel writers use present tense forms to record this incident (Mark 2:23; Luke 6:1). Nor is there any hint that the action was completed so that it was once for all, never to be done again. In the aorist tense the action occurs, with no notion of its beginning, duration, or conclusion.

This becomes clearer as we distinguish among the ordinary use of the aorist indicative, the special use of the aorist indicative, and the non-indicative use of the aorist.

3.1.1. Ordinary Usage of the Aorist Indicative

Beginning Greek students soon learn that aorist indicative forms all have an augment prefixed (typically ἐ-). This augment indicates past time; thus, aorist indicative forms mean simple action in the past time. This is true both for the first aorist, which is built on the present stem plus the -σα- suffix, and the second aorist, built on the aorist stem without the -σα- suffix.

FIRST AORIST	SECOND AORIST
ἔλυσα (λύω)	ἔλιπον (λείπω)
I loosed	I left

Grammarians call this ordinary use of the aorist by a variety of names: the **simple aorist**, the **unspecified aorist**, or the **constative aorist**. Some theorists have been very particular about distinguishing among various shades of this simple past action (inceptive aorist, constative aorist, culminative aorist). Do not waste your time deliberating this; little of sermonic value can be derived from it. You will do better to consider the nature of the verb stem itself.

For example, πιστεύω (I believe) in itself implies ongoing belief, as even a brief survey of Scripture indicates. The nature of faith is that it continues over a period of time (see Jas. 2 especially). By contrast, ἀποθνήσκω (I die) is something that happens at one point of time. Thus, compare the following aorist verbs.

καὶ ὁ ἄλλος μαθητὴς . . . **ἐπίστευσεν.**

And the other disciple . . . **believed** (John 20:8).

Χριστὸς **ἀπέθανεν** ὑπὲρ τῶν ἁμαρτιῶν ἡμῶν.

Christ **died** for our sins (1 Cor. 15:3).

In the first example, it is futile to make a point over whether, in this verse, the faith mentioned was once-for-all or inceptive or punctiliar or something else. The Evangelist is merely stating that faith followed the evidence of the empty tomb. Presumably such faith was strengthened and continued to grow, but this comes from recognizing the nature of the verb πιστεύω and from the sentences in John 20 that follow.

On the other hand, it is correct to refer to Christ's death as punctiliar or once-for-all. This is not true because 1 Corinthians

15:3 uses the aorist but because death itself is punctiliar. The Christian understanding that Christ's death was once-for-all is surely based on texts such as Hebrews 7:27, which specifically uses the Greek adverb ἐφάπαξ (once for all time) to point to the non-repeatable nature of Christ's death.

3.1.2. Special Uses of the Aorist Indicative

Most aorist indicatives in the New Testament refer to simple action in past time without any special sort of significance. Every page of the Greek Testament has many such examples. Fewer than 5% of aorist verbs are used in unexpected ways. These are all really Greek **idioms**, or expressions peculiar to New Testament Greek.

3.1.2.1. Proverbial aorist. General truths valid for all times are expressed in English in the present or future tenses. These may be proverbs: The early bird catches the worm; boys will be boys. They may be cultural observations: Preachers like fried chicken; fraternity men will party after the homecoming game. Although the Greek present and future tenses are most often used for such expressions, occasionally aorists are used for timeless truths. This is also called the gnomic aorist.

ἐὰν μὴ τις μένῃ ἐν ἐμοί, ἐβλήθη.

If someone does not remain in me, he **will be cast out** (John 15:6).

ἐξηράνθη ὁ χόρτος, καὶ τὸ ἄνθος ἐξέπεσεν.

Grass **withers**, and flowers **fall off** (1 Pet. 1:24).

The first example is proverbial as an enduring observation of Christianity, though theologians argue about its precise meaning. The second is proverbial as a common truth of human life. The aorist indicative is appropriate for each. To determine whether an aorist may be proverbial ask yourself: Is this statement reliable or true throughout long periods of time? Can the verb be translated well with an English present or future? If you answer yes to both questions, you probably have a proverbial aorist.

3.1.2.2. Futuristic aorist. Occasionally events yet to happen were thought of as so certain that the action was stated in the aorist. In the example that follows, so certainly will the apostles bear much fruit that the (future) glorification of the Father is expressed by an aorist verb. Notice that the English rendering requires the future (or present) indicative. A past tense English translation does not work.

ἐν τούτῳ ἐδοξάσθη ὁ πατήρ μου, ἵνα καρπὸν πολὺν φέρητε.

By this my Father **will be glorified**, that you bear much fruit (John 15:8).

Some commentators include the following example from Paul. Notice again that—contrary to most English versions—a future translation is more adequate than a past tense rendering.

οὓς δὲ ἐδικαίωσεν, τούτους καὶ **ἐδόξασεν.**

And the ones he justified, those also he **will glorify** (Rom. 8:30).

Sentences with aorist main verbs connected with an implied or stated condition are sometimes futuristic aorist statements. Both examples cited above may be recast into conditional forms: "If you (apostles) will bear much fruit, then my Father will be glorified; if He (God) will justify people, then He also will glorify them." A rule of thumb is to ask: Is this aorist statement reliable or true for some point future from when it was spoken? Can the statement be put into a conditional form? If you can answer these yes, you probably have a futuristic aorist.

3.1.2.3. Literary aorist. When you are writing a letter, English custom requires that you refer to actions connected with your writing activity in the present tense. You use the present because the activities are present to you: "Dear Sue, I am writing to tell you about my accident. I am sending this note through Mary, who will be passing by your house." In such situations Greek idiom used aorist verbs because by the time the letter was read, the action was already past; the reader's perspective rather than the writer's determined the tense. The **literary aorist** is sometimes called the **epistolary aorist.**

ἐγὼ Παῦλος **ἔγραψα** τῇ ἐμῇ χειρί.

I Paul **am writing** with my own hand (Philem. 19).

ἀναγκαῖον δὲ **ἡγησάμην** Ἐπαφρόδιτον . . . πέμψαι.

But I **consider** it necessary . . . to send Epaphroditus (Phil. 2:25).

A good rule is to ask: Is this aorist statement in an epistle? Was the action present to the author as he composed? If you answer yes, you probably have a literary aorist. Correct English idiom requires the present tense.

3.1.3. Aorist Non-indicative

The aorist was frequently used outside the indicative mood. Almost every page of the New Testament has examples of aorist verbs that are non-indicative but finite (subjunctive, imperative, or optative) or non-indicative as well as non-finite (participle or infinitive). For these, the fact that the tense is aorist usually has no special meaning. The action is no longer in past time (indicated by the lack of augment in all such forms). The action is simply looked at as a whole. All such aorists are unspecified or **simple aorists.** An example of each of the five possiblities illumines this.

SUBJUNCTIVE: τί **φάγωμεν**; ἤ· τί **πίωμεν**;

"What **should we eat?**" or, "What **should we drink?**" (Matt. 6:31).

IMPERATIVE: **ἁγιασθήτω** τὸ ὄνομά σου.

Hallowed be your name (Matt. 6:10).

OPTATIVE: ναὶ, ἀδελφέ, ἐγώ σου **ὀναίμην** ἐν κυρίῳ.

Yes, brother, **let** me **benefit** in the Lord from you (Philem. 20).

INFINITIVE: καὶ ἤλθομεν **προσκυνῆσαι** αὐτῷ.

And we came **to worship** him (Matt. 2:2).

PARTICIPLE: εἰ πνεῦμα ἅγιον ἐλάβετε **πιστεύσαντες**;

Did you receive the Holy Spirit **when you believed?** (Acts 19:2).

For each of these, the action expressed in the aorist may have happened over a long period of time. The aorists above summarize activities like eating, drinking, or hallowing. Nothing else may be learned.

Prohibition. When second person aorist subjunctives are preceded by the negative μή, the action is prohibited from taking place. It is a negative command.

μὴ **φοβηθῆτε** ἀπὸ τῶν ἀποκτεινόντων τὸ σῶμα.

Don't **ever fear** from the ones who kill the body (Luke 12:4).

Emphatic denial. When aorist subjunctives are preceded by the negative οὐ μή, the action becomes emphatic. In a statement, this is a strong denial that the action can ever occur. In a question, it is a way of affirming that the action will surely happen (sections 4.2.1.2 and 4.2.1.3).

οὐ μὴ **ἀδικηθῇ** ἐκ τοῦ θανάτου τοῦ δευτέρου.

He **will** never **be hurt** by the second death (Rev. 2:11).

οὐ μὴ **πίω** αὐτῷ;

Must I not **drink** it? (John 18:11).

Aorist and time. It has sometimes been thought that action indicated in aorist participles always occurred before the action indicated by the main verb. In fact, context must determine this. In Acts 19:2, the main verb is aorist, but the aorist participle indicates an action current with the time of the main verb. On the other hand, an aorist participle sometimes indicates time that is relatively prior. This is inherent in the context, but not in the aorist participle. Remember that outside the indicative, the aorist was timeless. In the following example, common sense—not the aorist participle—determines the sequence.

ἤγειρεν αὐτὴν **κρατήσας** τῆς χειρός.

After taking her hand he raised her up (Mark 1:31).

3.1.4. Summary of the Aorist

By now you should be convinced that most aorists are not worth mentioning from the pulpit.

1. The vast majority of aorist indicatives are simple statements of past action. Assume this for any given aorist indicative unless application of rules of thumb suggests an exception. The few exceptions are the proverbial, the futuristic, and the literary aorist. These idioms need to be translated into the correct English tense.

2. Aorist non-indicatives are statements of simple action without reference to time. Certain constructions, notably the aorist subjunctive preceded by μή or οὐ μή have special emphasis and may deserve sermonic attention. On the other hand, aorist participles in themselves must also be seen as statements of simple action.

3.2. Present

The present tense ordinarily suggests 41 some idea of continuous action. To conceptualize the present, think of a line; the present is often called a linear tense. Action in a present tense form is action in progress. There is no statement as to whether the action was ever completed, only that it had a point of beginning and some kind of continuance, at least for a period of time. Only in present indicative forms is any sense of present time involved.

3.2.1. Main Usage of the Present Indicative

Present indicative verbs depict action in progress at the present time. Present indicative verbs are like a tape made by a video camera; aorist indicative verbs are like the picture an instant-print camera produces. "He is building a house" states the process; "he built a house" summarizes a long sequence of building events.

The Greek present is sometimes formed by using the present of εἰμί (to be) accompanied by a present participle (see John 1:41 for an example). This construction is called the present **periphrastic**. This is similar to the English alternatives "he builds" (simple present) or "he is building" (periphrastic present).

The main use of the present indicative is usually called the **descriptive present**. When the activity is clearly ongoing, it may be further classified as descriptive-continuous.

ἀλήθειαν **λέγω** ἐν Χριστῷ, οὐ **ψεύδομαι.**

I am speaking the truth in Christ, **I am** not **lying** (Rom. 9:1).

διδάσκαλε, οὐ **μέλει** σοι ὅτι **ἀπολλύμεθα;**

Teacher, **do** you not **care** that **we are perishing**? (Mark 4:38).

Some descriptive present indicatives carry a slightly different notion, but this is due to the nature of the verb root or the context rather than anything to do with tense.

Some activities are not so much continuous as they are repetitive. Eating or sleeping do not ordinarily go on without ceasing, yet someone may easily say, I sleep eight hours a night or I eat bananas with my corn flakes. Grammarians call this the **iterative present**; some descriptive present verbs may be called descriptive-iterative. In English, we often translate this "keep on [ask]ing."

νηστεύω δὶς τοῦ σαββάτου.

I keep on fasting twice a week (Luke 18:12).

Other activities in the present take only a brief moment. They are truly descriptive but they are further defined as the **punctiliar present** or descriptive-punctiliar. Common sense points out that such may be the case. There was no other way to say this in Greek except by a present indicative.

ἀφίενταί σου αἱ ἁμαρτίαι.

Your sins **are forgiven** you (Mark 2:5).

The classification **descriptive present** is usually sufficient. There is no point in trying to distinguish descriptive-continuous, descriptive-iterative, or descriptive-punctiliar. People generally do a good job at intuitively recognizing such distinctions without drawing it to their attention. In any case, there is rarely sermonic value in noting such distinctions.

3.2.2. Special Uses of the Present Indicative

3.2.2.1. Historical present. Greek, English, and many other languages use the present tense, especially in colloquial speech or slang, to relate events of the past. Stories told this way tend to be quite vivid. Consider the following: "Now Fox is mighty tired of being fooled by Rabbit. So he says to Bear, 'We gotta have us a plan.'" English typically limits this to folk tales and fables, but in Greek this was a great way to tell about real events. The Gospels of John and Mark used the historical present. One wonders whether these Evangelists were replaying their mind's videotape of the event as they wrote. The *New American Standard Bible* notes historical present verbs with an asterisk. In the following examples, the English verbs have been put into past time because that is what English speakers expect when serious history is being related.

καὶ **εἰσπορεύονται** εἰς Καφαρναούμ.

And **they went** into Capernaum (Mark 1:21).

ἔρχεται γυνὴ ἐκ τῆς Σαμαρειίας ἀντλῆσαι ὕδωρ.

A Samaritan woman **came** to draw water (John 4:7).

A good guideline is to ask: Was the present tense used to relate a story or a historical narrative? Was this used mainly for literary effect? If you answer these yes, you probably have a historical present. English idiom requires the past tense.

3.2.2.2. Proverbial present. Review the material about the proverbial aorist (section 3.1.2.1.). The present tense was commonly used to express timeless truth. Unlike the ordinary present, proverbial action is not necessarily happening right now. Sometimes this is called the gnomic present. A good way to determine whether a present is proverbial is to ask: Is this statement reliable or true throughout long periods of time? If you answer yes, you probably have a proverbial present, for which the English present tense is perfectly acceptable.

ἕκαστος δὲ **πειράζεται** ὑπὸ τῆς ἰδίας ἐπιθυμίας.

But each person **is tempted** by his own lusts (Jas. 1:14).

οὐδεὶς προφήτης δεκτός **ἐστιν** ἐν τῇ πατρίδι αὐτοῦ.

No prophet **is** welcome in his homeland (Luke 4:24).

3.2.2.3. Futuristic present. The futuristic present is similar to the **futuristic aorist** (see section 3.1.2.2.). Actions that are certain to occur may be thought of as going on at the time of speaking, at least in the speaker's mind. This is common in both Greek and English. Every native English speaker understands that the statement "My grandmother is coming for Christmas" refers to future time. So it is in Greek. Those familiar with southern English dialect recognize this as like the idiom "fixing to" or "going to" followed by an infinitive. A good rule of thumb is to ask: Does this statement evidently look to some future point from the time it was spoken? If you answer these yes, you probably have a futuristic present.

ἴδε **ἄγω** ὑμῖν αὐτὸν ἔξω.

Look, **I will bring** him to you outside (John 19:4).

SOUTHERN: Look, I'm **fixing to bring** him to you outside.

Αἰνέα, **ἰᾶταί** σε Ἰησοῦ.

Aeneas, Jesus **will heal** you (Acts 9:34).

SOUTHERN: Aeneas, Jesus **is fixing to heal** you.

A slight variation of this is the futuristic present in which the action is not certain to occur but only predicted or intended. Some grammarians call this special present tense the attempted or **conative present**.

διὰ ποῖον αὐτῶν ἔργον ἐμὲ **λιθάζετε**;

For which work of these **do you intend to stone** me? (John 10:32).

3.2.3. Present Non-indicative

The Greek present tense is often used outside the indicative mood. Just as with the aorist non-indicative, the pages of the New Testament abound with examples. These include present verbs that are not indicative but finite (subjunctive, imperative, or optative). They also include those that are present but neither indicative nor finite (participle or infinitive). For these the action is not present time any more. The action is seen as a process. The action is assumed to occur over a period of time—either continuously or iteratively—but nothing is implied about whether the action has been finished or not. Often the translation "kept on" shows the continuous nature of the actions. This contrasts with aorist non-indicatives, for which nothing is said about the duration of the action. Consider an example of each of the five.

SUBJUNCTIVE: τοῦτο προσεύχομαι, ἵνα ἡ ἀγάπη ὑμῶν
. . . **περισσεύῃ**.

I pray this, that your love. . . **will keep on abounding** (Phil. 1:9).

IMPERATIVE: **βλέπετε** τοὺς κακοὺς ἐργάτας.

Keep on looking out for the evil workers (Phil. 3:2).

OPTATIVE: εἰ καὶ **πάσχοιτε** διὰ δικαιοσύνην.

Even if **you keep on suffering** for righteousness (1 Pet. 3:14).

INFINITIVE: ἤρξατο ὁ Ἰησοῦ **κηρύσσειν** καὶ **λέγειν**.

Jesus began **to be preaching** and **to be saying** (Matt. 4:17).

PARTICIPLE: **περιπατῶν** δὲ. . . εἶδεν δύο ἀδελφούς.

And **while he was walking**. . . he saw two brothers (Matt. 4:18).

For each of these, the action expressed by the present tense clearly implies some process or period of time involved. The example from Philippians 1:9 is clearly a continuous process, while the Matthew 4:17 example is certainly an iterative process, but observing such a distinction is not helpful. In the sentences in which they stand, the verbs are present to draw attention to the process. The best way to indicate this in English depends on the individual sentence.

Negative command. Two constructions call for special mention. First, when **present imperatives** are preceded by a form of the negative μή, the action is usually assumed to be going on, but must stop. It is a negative command, a call to end an action. (Compare this to the aorist subjunctive plus μή [section 3.1.3.].)

εἴ τις οὐ θέλει ἐργάζεσθαι μηδὲ **ἐσθιέτω**.

If someone isn't willing to work, **let him stop eating** (2 Thess. 3:10).

μὴ **φοβοῦ**.

Quit **being afraid** (Rev. 1:17).

Process and common sense. Some have thought that present participles generally indicate action of the same time as the main verb. Often this is true, as in the example of Matthew 4:18 cited above. On the other hand, sometimes a present participle indicates a relatively later time, but that is not inherent and must be determined from the context.

οἱ ἀδελφοὶ αὐτοῦ. . . ἀπέστειλαν πρὸς αὐτὸν **καλοῦντες** αὐτον.

His brothers. . . sent (someone) to him **calling** him (Mark 3:31).

Clearly the calling followed the sending. Remember that outside the indicative, the present merely indicates process. In the following example, common sense determines that the sequence is seeing first and rewarding second.

ὁ πατήρ σου ὁ **βλέπων**. . . ἀποδώσει σοι.

Your Father who **keeps seeing**. . . will reward you (Matt. 6:18).

3.2.4 Summary of the Present

Often, present tense verbs are worth mentioning in a sermon, especially when the English version you use does not convey a sense of the continuing action of the present.

1. Most present indicatives are simple statements describing action that goes on over a period of time. Assume that the present forms you encounter are descriptive unless the guidelines indicate otherwise. Do not try to distinguish continuous, iterative, or punctiliar varieties of such descriptive presents.

2. Historical presents rarely call for sermonic comment since most modern English versions render them correctly in past time. Proverbial presents seldom call for comment either, unless you must call attention to the statement as proverbial. Since futuristic

presents have a fairly close parallel in English, they do not usually call for any explanation.

3. All present non-indicatives are statements of continuing action without reference to time. Certain constructions, notably the present imperative preceded by μή, have special emphasis and deserve mention. On the other hand, present participles simply state continuing action, but context and common sense determine the time of action in relation to the main verb.

3.3. Perfect

Now we turn to the tense with more theological and sermonic value than any other. The perfect tense carries the idea of completed action; this is true of both indicative and non-indicative forms. Perfect action is already complete but its effects last into the present. This goes beyond the English perfect, which carries with it only the idea of completed action. To conceptualize the perfect, think of a filled-in circle followed by a line: ●————. The action indicated by a perfect tense form is finished or "perfected." In perfect indicative forms, the action has been completed and continues to the present time of the writer. For this reason, what we usually call the Greek perfect tense may even better be called the present perfect tense.

3.3.1. Main Usage of the Perfect Indicative

As a beginning Greek student, you learned that all forms of the perfect, whether indicative or not, use reduplication. Such reduplication draws attention to the completed action that perfect forms invariably communicate. The vast majority of perfect indicatives in the New Testament fall into the category of **pure perfects**, also called the **consummative perfect**. This is the normal sense of the perfect tense: a completed action has had a lasting effect.

πεπληρώκατε τὴν Ἰερουσαλὴμ τῆς διδαχῆς ὑμῶν.

You have filled Jerusalem with your teaching (Acts 5:28).

τὸν καλὸν ἀγῶνα **ἠγώνισμαι**.

I have fought the good fight (2 Tim. 4:7).

As you can see from these examples, the customary English translation for the perfect uses "has" or "have." This is an approximation. (English speakers do not ordinarily perceive that continuing results are included in the action of the verb.) With perfect passive verbs, however, a more satisfactory English rendering is often possible. In the following examples, the "better" translations show how Greek perfect passives can be more adequately rendered.

ὁ δὲ μὴ πιστεύων ἤδη **κέκριται**.

GOOD: But the one not believing **has been condemned** already (John 3:18).

BETTER: But the one not believing **is condemned** already.

γέγραπται, Κύριον τὸν θεόν σου προσκυνήσεις.

GOOD: **It has been written,** "Worship the Lord your God" (Luke 4:8).

BETTER: **It is written,** "Worship the Lord your God."

These "better" translations do in some sense communicate that the effects of the action continue. You may want to point this out in a preaching context.

The Greek perfect is sometimes formed by using the present of eijmiv accompanied by a perfect participle (see Eph. 2:8 for an example). Such a Greek construction, referred to as a perfect **periphrastic**, is a matter of stylistic preference but has no exegetical significance.

3.3.2. Special Uses of the Perfect Indicative

Two special kinds of perfects are occasionally found. Again, this is simply a place where Greek usage differed from English and must be treated accordingly.

3.3.2.1. Intensive perfect. The perfect of certain verbs focused on the existing result of an action. In some cases these came to approximate the English present tense; the most common example of this is the verb οἶδα, always translated "know" rather than "have known." Other verbs that usually have such an intensive sense are ἕστηκα (I stand), πέποιθα (I am persuaded), μέμνημαι (I remember), τέθηνκα (I am dead), and πέπεισμαι (I am convinced). Some grammarians broaden the **intensive perfect** to include verbs of seeing, knowing, understanding, and believing, although others are reluctant to go this far. A good guideline for checking whether a perfect might be intensive is to ask: Is this verb in the list above? Is the focus of the verb clearly on the present time rather than on the completed results? Can the verb be translated as an English present? If you answer yes to these questions, you probably have an intensive perfect, best translated as an English present.

καὶ πᾶς μὲν ἱερεὺς **ἕστηκεν** καθ᾽ ἡμέραν.

And indeed every priest **stands** daily (Heb. 10:11).

3.3.2.2. Historical perfect. The historical perfect is like the **historical present** (see 3.2.2.1). Historical perfects narrate historical events using the perfect rather than the more typical aorist. This was another way Greek speakers had of vividly telling about the past, best rendered by the simple past in English. A good rule of thumb in checking whether a perfect is historical is to ask: Is the perfect tense used to relate a story or a historical narrative? Is this used mainly for purposes of literary effect? If you answer yes, you have a historical perfect.

εὑρὼν δὲ ἕνα πολύτιμον μαργαρίτην. . . **πέπρακεν** πάντα.

And when he found one valuable pearl. . . **he sold** everything (Matt. 13:46).

Both historical and intensive perfects need to be recognized and properly translated. Neither calls for special attention in a sermon.

3.3.3. Perfect Non-indicative

Although perfect forms outside the indicative are found in the Greek Testament, they are not so frequent as aorist and present non-indicative forms. The New Testament has no perfect opatives. The perfect imperative is exceedingly rare. The perfect subjunctive is usually formed by a **periphrastic**. The major exception is εἰδῶ, the subjunctive of οἶδα, functioning as a present subjunctive. This means that you need be acquainted only with the perfect subjunctive, the perfect infinitive (also rare), and the perfect participle. For each of these, the main point is always completed action. An example of each of these three illustrates this.

SUBJUNCTIVE: αἰτεῖτε. . . ἵνα ἡ χαρὰ ὑμῶν **ᾖ πεπληρωμένη**.

Ask. . . so that your joy **may be fulfilled** (John 16:24).

INFINITIVE: διὰ τὸ **διατεταχέναι** Κλαύδιον χωρίζεσθαι πάντας τοὺς. . . Ἰουδαίους ἀπὸ τῆς Ῥώμης.

Because Claudius **had ordered** all the Jews to leave Rome (Acts 18:2).

PARTICIPLE: πάντα τὰ **γεγραμμένα** ἐν τῷ νόμῳ Μωϋσέως.

Everything **which is written** in the Law of Moses (Luke 24:44).

For each of these, the English rendering has to be adjusted for correct style, but the main consideration is that an action has been completed, with ongoing results.

3.3.4. Summary of the Perfect

Many perfect forms deserve mention in your sermons.

1. Most perfect indicatives, the pure perfects, indicate action that is complete, with results going on to the time of speaking or writing. Assume that the perfects you encounter fall into this category unless there are strong reasons for thinking otherwise. A few, called **intensive perfects** (οἶδα and several others), place the emphasis on present time only and should be translated by the En-

glish present. Those used in narrative for effect (**historical perfects**) should be rendered by the English past.

2. Perfect non-indicatives generally emphasize completed action (except for forms of οἶδα). The most frequent of these are the perfect participles.

3.4. Future

The future tense is like the aorist as far as the kind of action is concerned. That is, it represents simple or unspecified action. To conceptualize the future, think of a small circle (as we did for the aorist). The future tense tells nothing about whether the action will be completed or terminated, nor is anything included about the beginning or the process of the action. This is really a matter of common sense: since the future is basically unknown, who can say what the kind of action is?

The Greek future is sometimes formed by using the future of εἰμί accompanied by a present participle (see Luke 21:17 for an example) or by a form of μέλλω plus an infintive (note John 12:33). This is similar to the English alternatives "he will build" or "he is going to build." Such constructions, referred to as future **periphrastics**, are a matter of stylistic preference.

3.4.1. Main Usage of the Future Indicative

The future indicative predicts that an action or event will occur at some future point. This is precisely like the English future. It is usually called the **predictive future**, although some grammarians call it the **prophetic future**. There is rarely any value in trying to distinguish such forms as to whether they are punctiliar or linear. Most future indicatives merely mean future time. Nothing is said about whether the predicted action actually happened later.

ἄλλον παράκλητον **δώσει** ὑμῖν.

He will give you another Counselor (John 14:16).

πέποιθα δὲ ἐν κυρίῳ ὅτι καὶ αὐτὸς ταχέως **ἐλεύσομαι.**

I am persuaded in the Lord that **I will come** soon (Phil. 2:24).

In the first example the action was fulfilled by the events of Acts 2, which further points to the action as point-of-time rather than ongoing. This is determined by Acts 2, not John 14:16. In the second example, there is no way of knowing whether Paul's prediction ever came true.

3.4.2. Special Uses of the Future Indicative

Future indicative forms can be used in two idiomatic ways, both of which have rather close parallels in English.

3.4.2.1. Proverbial future. Go back and read again the material about the proverbial aorist (section 3.1.2.1.). The future is well suited as a tense for stating that which typically will occur. Sometimes these are called **gnomic** or **aphoristic futures**. In English either the future or the present tense translates this **idiom**.

ἡ ἀλήθεια **ἐλευθερώσει** ὑμᾶς.

FUTURE: Truth **will free** you (John 8:32).

PRESENT: Truth **frees** you.

μοιχαλὶς **χρηματίσει** ἐὰν γένηται ἀνδρὶ ἑτέρῳ.

FUTURE: **She will be called** an adulteress
if she takes another husband (Rom. 7:3).

PRESENT: **She is called** an adulteress if she takes another husband.

A good way to check whether a future form might be proverbial is to ask: Is this statement reliable or true throughout long periods of time? Can the verb be translated as either an English present or future? If you answer yes to both questions, you probably have a proverbial future.

3.4.2.2. Imperative future. The ordinary way to express a command in Greek is by the imperative mood. However, this is equally well expressed by a second person future indicative. In English it makes little difference whether I tell my son, "Study your math homework tonight" or "You shall study your math homework tonight." Each of the following can be rendered by a present imperative or by a future command. Some grammarians call this the **volitional future.**

καλέσεις τὸ ὄνομα αὐτοῦ . . . Ἰησοῦν.

PRESENT IMPERATIVE: **Call** his name Jesus (Matt. 1:21).

FUTURE COMMAND: **You shall call** his name Jesus.

ἀγαπήσεις τὸν πλησίον σου ὡς σεαυτόν.

PRESENT IMPERATIVE: **Love** your neighbor as yourself (Jas. 2:8).

FUTURE COMMAND: **You shall love** your neighbor as yourself.

A good rule of thumb in checking whether a future form might be imperative is to ask: Is this second person? Is this best understood as a command? If you answer yes to both questions, you probably have an imperative future.

3.4.2.3. Perfect future. Rarely in any language is there need to refer to action that will be completed in the future. However, one can think of such situations. For example, "By this time next month we will have finished our study of Greek." In the Greek Testament, this is accomplished in a **periphrastic** way, by combining a future form of εἰμί and a perfect participle. Such a construction is to be translated like an ordinary perfect plus "shall" or "will" to move the action to the future.

ὅσα ἐὰν λύσητε ἐπὶ τῆς γῆς **ἔσται λελυμένα** ἐν οὐρανῷ.

Whatever you loose on earth **will have been loosed** in heaven (Matt. 18:18).

On the rare occasions when you encounter this kind of construction, the writer or speaker had in mind an event or action to be completed in the future. This may require special sermonic focus, for this is not evident in most English version renderings.

3.4.3. Future Non-indicative

Greek never had a future imperative. Neither the future subjunctive nor the future optative is found in the New Testament. This leaves only the future infinitive and the future participle. Typically they were used to express the purpose or aim of another action. They also refer to a time future to the main verb.

INFINITIVE: ὤμοσεν μὴ **εἰσελεύσεσθαι** εἰς τὴν κατάπαυσιν αὐτοῦ.

He swore that **they would** not **enter** his rest (Heb. 3:18).

PARTICIPLE: ὃς ἐληλύθει **προσκυνήσων** εἰς . . . Ἰερουσαλήμ.

Who had come to Jerusalem **to worship** (Acts 8:27).

3.4.4. Summary of the Future

As you have learned, most future forms are not worth special mention in a sermon.

1. In Greek the ordinary future simply predicts an action, just as in English. This calls for correctly translating the Greek into an equivalent English verb. Assume that the Greek future forms you encounter are of this sort unless there is strong reason to think otherwise.

2. The imperative future may be worth sermonic mention, especially when one is dealing with a command still applicable to believers of today. The proverbial future, like proverbial aorists and presents, mainly requires recognition that the statement is something that does happen rather than something the speaker wishes to have happen. The perfect future works much like the ordinary perfect, but the completion of action is anticipated, not already accomplished.

3. The few future forms found outside the indicative call attention both to purpose and to action subsequent to the time of the main verb.

3.5. Imperfect

Just as the future is a special type of aorist, the imperfect is a special type of present. The imperfect is the present removed to the past. This is especially obvious because the imperfect stem is formed by adding an augment (the sign of the past) to the present stem.

PRESENT	IMPERFECT
λύω	ἔλυον
I am loosing	I was loosing

Like the present, the imperfect signifies action in progress (3.2.1). The imperfect was used when such action occurred in the past, much as a video camera records. This tense is never used outside the indicative, but it is occasionally formed by the imperfect **periphrastic** construction of the imperfect of εἰμί, plus a present participle (for example, Luke 1:21).

3.5.1. Main Usage of the Imperfect Indicative

The imperfect usually describes an action that unfolded during some past time. Grammarians usually call this the **descriptive imperfect**. Most imperfect verbs fall into this category, and the English rendering "was [ask]ing" or "were [ask]ing" is usually adequate for the active; "was being [ask]ed" or "were being [asked]" usually accomodates the passive.

ἡ δὲ πενθερὰ Σίμωνος **κατέκειτο** πυρέσσουσα.

But Simon's mother-in-law **was lying** with a fever (Mark 1:30).

καὶ οἱ μὲν **ἐπείθοντο** τοῖς λεγομένοις.

And some **were being persuaded** by the things said (Acts 28:24).

Some descriptive imperfects, due to the nature of the action or the context, imply repeated action. These **iterative imperfects** are best designated as descriptive-iterative. You may want to read again the discussion at the end of section 3.2.1. In English, the idioms "kept on [ask]ing" or "used to [ask]" accomodate this idea.

ἐπορεύοντο οἱ γονεῖς αὐτοῦ κατ᾽ ἔτος εἰς Ἰερουσαλήμ.

His parents **used to go** every year to Jerusalem (Luke 2:41).

ὕδατα πολλὰ ἦν ἐκεῖ, καὶ **παρεγίνοντο** καὶ **ἐβαπτίζοντο**.

Much water was there, and people **kept going out
and kept on being baptized** (John 3:23).

3.5.2. Special Uses of the Imperfect Indicative

The imperfect is used occasionally in situations that are not self-evident to English speakers. These are the inceptive and the inferential imperfect idioms.

3.5.2.1. Inceptive imperfect. Any action that goes on for a period of time in the past has a beginning point. Although there is a way to emphasize beginning (a form of ἄρχομαι plus an infinitive), sometimes an ordinary imperfect carries this sense. The English rendering "began [ask]ing" is a good representation of this. The *New American Standard Bible* notes inceptive imperfects by italicizing the word *began*.

ἀνοίαξας τὸ στόμα αὐτοῦ **ἐδίδασκεν** αὐτούς.

When he opened his mouth **he began teaching** them (Matt. 5:2).

A good rule of thumb is to ask: Does this imperfect verb seem to emphasize the beginning of an action that went on for a time? If you answer yes, you probably have an inceptive imperfect. The English idiom translation uses "began." As a rule this need not be commented on in a sermonic context.

3.5.2.2. Inferential imperfect. Sometimes Greek conditional sentences deal with historical situations in which something could have happened but did not (second class conditionals, see 4.1.2.3 and 4.7.1.2). In English such hypothetical situations are easy to follow: "If John had majored in business instead of history, he would be wealthy today." English uses "could" or "would" in the conclusion; the Greek uses the untranslatable word ἄν followed by the imperfect.

εἰ ἐκ τοῦ κόσμου ἦτε, ὁ κόσμος ἄν τὸ ἴδιον **ἐφίλει**.

If you were from the world,
the world **would be loving** its own (John 15:19).

Remember that an imperfect verb following ἄν in a conditional sentence is making an inference that is not actual. English translation requires "could" or "would."

3.5.3. Summary of the Imperfect

Translating the imperfect carefully is the key to understanding the original text. All imperfect forms carry with them some emphasis on linear action in past time. Usually you need not distinguish descriptive-iterative imperfects from ordinary descriptive imperfects, although translation with "kept on" or "used to" is helpful. Both inceptive imperfects and inferential imperfects may be dealt with by recognizing these idioms and translating them into the correct English equivalent.

3.6. Pluperfect.

The pluperfect is an auxiliary to the perfect, just as the the imperfect is an auxiliary to the present. The pluperfect carries the same sense as the perfect, but in past time. The pluperfect is formed by adding an augment to the reduplicated perfect stem.

PERFECT	PLUPERFECT
λέλυκα	ἐλελύκειν
I have loosed	I had loosed

Like the imperfect, it is used only in the indicative mood and is usually found in narrative contexts. The pluperfect **periphrastic** is made by combining the imperfect of εἰμί with a perfect participle (for example, Luke 8:2).

3.6.1. Main Usage of the Pluperfect

Most pluperfects in the New Testament are called pure pluperfects (or consummative pluperfects). That is, they are similar to the indicative pure perfects, except that the time referred to is past (see 3.3.1). These pluperfects refer to a completed action, with results continuing up to some past time, usually a specific time referred to within the context. The best way to understand this is as follows: ●————|. The circle represents the completed action; the horizontal line suggests the continuing effect; and the little vertical line represents the past time referred to in the context. In English the translational equivalent is usually "had" plus the past participle, but this is only an approximation.

Whether the results of the pluperfect have continued beyond the time referred to in the narrative depends on the context. The use of the pluperfect means only that the results were in effect at the time of the narrative.

ἤδη γὰρ **συνετέθειντο** οἱ Ἰουδαῖοι.

For the Jews already **had agreed** (John 9:22).

Λάζαρος **ἐβέβλητο** πρὸς τὸν πυλῶνα.

Lazarus **had been laid** at the gate (Luke 16:20).

In each of these—the first active, the second passive—the effect of using the pluperfect is clear. An action had been accomplished; the action's effects continued; then some further development of the narrative unfolds.

3.6.2. Special Use of the Pluperfect Indicative

Do you remember the **intensive perfect**? If not, reread section 3.3.2.1. The **perfect tense verbs** that emphasize present results with little emphasis on past completed action retain this distinction for the pluperfect. That is, when these verbs occur in the pluperfect, they simply mean that something *was*. They are called **intensive pluperfects**. They are to be translated as simple past time.

ἐγὼ δὲ **ᾔδειν** ὅτι πάντοτέ μου ἀκούεις.

But I **knew** that you always hear me (John 11:42).

καὶ ἰδοὺ ἄνδρες δύω **παρειστήκεισαν**.

And behold, two men **stood** there (Acts 1:10).

In order to recognize this, you need to be acquainted with the verbs listed in section 3.3.2.1. When these occur in the pluperfect tense, they should be translated as if they were aorist.

3.6.3. Summary of the Pluperfect

Because pluperfect forms are most often used in narrative, they usually carry little theological significance (in contrast to the perfect). Neither **pure pluperfects** nor the less-common **intensive pluperfects** warrant much mention in a sermon.

Summary of Verb Tense

1. AORIST

SIMPLE (or UNSPECIFIED or CONSTATIVE)	=	indicative main use
PROVERBIAL (or GNOMIC)	=	indicative special use
FUTURISTIC	=	indicative special use
LITERARY (or EPISTOLARY)	=	indicative special use
UNSPECIFIED (or SIMPLE)	=	non-indicative use
SUBJUNCTIVE plus μή or οὐ μή	=	non-indicative special use

2. PRESENT

DESCRIPTIVE (subcategories: CON-TINUOUS, ITERATIVE, PUNCTILIAR)	=	indicative main use
HISTORICAL	=	indicative special use
PROVERBIAL (or GNOMIC)	=	indicative special use
FUTURISTIC (subcategory: CONATIVE)	=	indicative special use
PROCESS	=	non-indicative use
IMPERATIVE plus μή	=	non-indicative special use

3. PERFECT

PURE (or CONSUMMATIVE)	=	indicative main use
INTENSIVE	=	indicative special use
HISTORICAL	=	indicative special use
PURE (or CONSUMMATIVE)	=	non-indicative use

4. FUTURE

PREDICTIVE (or PROPHETIC)	=	indicative main use
PROVERBIAL (or GNOMIC or APHORISTIC)	=	indicative special use
IMPERATIVE (or VOLITIONAL)	=	indicative special use
PERFECT	=	indicative special use
PURPOSE	=	non-indicative use

5. IMPERFECT

DESCRIPTIVE (subcategory: ITERATIVE)	=	indicative main use
INCEPTIVE	=	indicative special use
INFERENTIAL	=	indicative special use

6. PLUPERFECT

PURE (or CONSUMMATIVE)	=	indicative main use
INTENSIVE	=	indicative special use

For Further Reading

Blass, F., and A. Debrunner. *A Greek Grammar of the New Testament and Other Early Christian Literature*, 166–81. Trans. and rev. Robert W. Funk. University of Chicago Press, 1961.

Brooks, James A., and Carlton L. Winbery. *Syntax of New Testament Greek*, 75–99. Washington: University Press of America, 1979.

Burton, Ernest de Witt. *Syntax of the Moods and Tenses in New Testament Greek*, 6–72. Edinburgh: T. & T. Clark, 1898.

Carson, D. A. *Exegetical Fallacies*, 67–90. Grand Rapids: Baker Book House, 1984.

Dana, H. E., and Julius R. Mantey. *A Manual Grammar of the Greek New Testament*, 176–208. New York: Macmillan Co., 1927.

MacDonald, William G. *Greek Enchiridion: A Concise Handbook of Grammar for Translation and Exegesis*, 3–40. Peabody, Mass.: Hendrickson Publishers, 1986.

Moule, C. F. D. *An Idiom Book of New Testament Greek,* 2nd ed., 5–19. Cambridge University Press, 1959.

Moulton, James Hope. *A Grammar of New Testament Greek.* Vol. 3, *Syntax*, by Nigel Turner, 59–89. Edinburgh: T. & T. Clark, 1963.

Robertson, A. T. *A Grammar of the Greek New Testament in the Light of Historical Research,* 343–67, 821–910. Nashville: Broadman, 1934.

Now Let's Apply

All verb forms from Matthew 4:1–11 and Philippians 1:3–11 are reproduced below, with tense and mood listed beside each. Determine what the tense significance is for each one. Indicate by writing yes or no whether you believe this particular verb is worth mention in a sermon. The first two verbs for each text have been completed to get you started.

Matthew 4

VERB	TENSE/ MOOD	TENSE SIGNIFICANCE	SERMON MENTION?
Verse 1:			
ἀνήχθη	aorist indicative	simple	no
πειρασθῆναι	aorist infinitive	unspecified	no
Verse 2:			
νηστεύσας	aorist participle	_____	_____
ἐπείνασεν	aorist indicative	_____	_____
Verse 3:			
προσελθὼν	aorist participle	_____	_____
πειράζων	present participle	_____	_____
εἶπεν	aorist indicative	_____	_____

εἶ   present
indicative

  _____   _____

εἰπέ   aorist
imperative

  _____   _____

γένωνται   aorist
subjunctive

  _____   _____

Verse 4:

ἀποκριθείς   aorist
participle

  _____   _____

εἶπεν   aorist
indicative

  _____   _____

γέγραπται   perfect
indicative

  _____   _____

ζήσεται   future
indicative

  _____   _____

ἐκπορευομένῳ   present
participle

  _____   _____

Verse 5:

παραλαμβάνει   present
indicative

  _____   _____

ἔστησεν   aorist
indicative

  _____   _____

Verse 6:

λέγει   present
indicative

  _____   _____

εἶ   present
indicative

  _____   _____

βάλε   aorist
imperative

  _____   _____

γέγραπται   perfect
indicative

  _____   _____

ἐντελεῖται   future
                indicative

_____ _____

ἀροῦσίν   future
                indicative

_____ _____

προσκόψῃς   aorist
                subjunctive

Verse 7:

_____ _____

ἔφη   aorist
                indicative

_____ _____

γέγραπται   perfect
                indicative

_____ _____

ἐκπειράσεις   future
                indicative

Verse 8:

_____ _____

παραλαμβάνει   present
                indicative

_____ _____

δείκνυσιν   present
                indicative

Verse 9:

_____ _____

εἶπεν   aorist
                indicative

_____ _____

δώσω   future
                indicative

_____ _____

πεσὼν   aorist
                participle

_____ _____

προσκυνήσῃς   aorist
                subjunctive

Verse 10:

_____ _____

λέγει   present
                indicative

_____ _____

ὕπαγε	present imperative	_____	_____
γέγραπται	perfect indicative	_____	_____
προσκυνήσεις	future indicative	_____	_____
λατρεύσεις	future indicative	_____	_____

Verse 11:

ἀφίησιν	present indicative	_____	_____
προσῆλθον	aorist indicative	_____	_____
διηκόνουν	aorist indicative	_____	_____

After you have completed the chart on Matthew 4:1–11, look back over your work. Underline the five verb forms that you think are most interesting from the point of view of tense and that you would consider giving sermonic attention. Can you justify your choices?

Philippians 1

VERB	TENSE/ MOOD	TENSE SIGNIFICANCE	SERMON MENTION?
Verse 3:			
εὐχαριστῶ	present indicative	descriptive	yes
Verse 4:			
ποιούμενος	present participle	*process*	yes

Verse 6:

πεποιθὼς   perfect
              participle   _____ _____

ἐναρξάμενος   aorist
               participle   _____ _____

ἐπιτελέσει   future
              indicative   _____ _____

Verse 7:

ἐστιν   present
         indicative   _____ _____

φρονεῖν   present
           infinitive   _____ _____

ἔχειν   present
        infinitive   _____ _____

ὄντας   present
         participle   _____ _____

Verse 8:

ἐπιποθῶ   present
           indicative   _____ _____

Verse 9:

προσεύχομαι   present
              indicative   _____ _____

περισσεύῃ   present
           subjunctive   _____ _____

Verse 10:

δοκιμάζειν   present
             infinitive   _____ _____

διαφέροντα   present
             participle   _____ _____

ἦτε   present
      subjunctive   _____ _____

Verse 11:

πεπληρωμένοι   perfect
            participle   _____   _____

After you have completed the chart on Philippians 1:3–11, look back over your work. Underline the five verb forms that you think are most interesting from the point of view of tense and that you would consider giving sermonic attention. Can you justify your choices?

Sanity About Moods

The Greek moods are usually easy to interpret. Like tense, appreciation of mood can help in sermon preparation. The trick is knowing when to bring out the contribution of a verb's mood. Mood tells whether—from the perspective of the speaker or writer—an action is actual or potential. Mood does not indicate whether such action is true or false, good or evil. It only tells the manner in which the action is related by the speaker or writer. Some grammarians use the term **mode** instead of mood; the terms are interchangeable.

English verbs contain mood information that native speakers understand intuitively. Consider the following examples.

Indicative	He **closes** the door.
Subjunctive	I asked that he **close** the door.
Imperative	**Close** the door.

A fairly sophisticated understanding of English grammar is needed to label these, yet even preschool children observe the distinctions. This chapter describes ways the Greek New Testament used mood. Through this information we can identify special emphases for sermon purposes. Mood only occasionally carries meaning worth noting in the pulpit.

Four moods are called true moods because all their forms have personal endings, such as first plural or third singular. That is, all forms of the true moods refer to a person, thing, or group specified by the personal ending or subject. The infinitive and participle are not limited by personal endings and are known as "near moods."

4.1. Indicative Mood

The indicative is the normal mood for speech and writing. It is found on every page of the Greek Testament and in every tense.

4.1.1. Ordinary Use of the Indicative

When you first learned about Greek verbs, you probably used only the indicative for a long time. Like the English indicative, the Greek **statement indicative** asserts that an action is real. Most indicatives are statement indicatives. Sermonic situations hardly require reference to this.

ὁ θεὸς **λαλήσας** τοῖς πατράσιν.

God **spoke** to the fathers (Heb. 1:1).

The writer uses the indicative to assert his belief that God really spoke. Like most indicative statements, this one is obvious.

4.1.2. Special Usage of the Indicative

Three specialized indicatives are found. Each of these has an English parallel. Only the second and third of these may require sermonic focus.

4.1.2.1. Interrogative indicative. When speakers ask for factual information, they normally use the indicative. This is true both for English and Greek and does not merit sermonic mention.

ὑμεῖς δὲ τίνα με **λέγετε** εἶναι;

But who **do** you **say** that I am? (Matt. 16:15).

ἔξεστιν δοῦναι κῆνσον Καίσαρι ἢ οὔ;

Is it lawful to pay taxes to Caesar or not? (Matt. 22:17).

Questions of this kind expect a straightforward answer. In the first example, the answer is, You are the Messiah. The second obviously expects yes or no. For other kinds of questions, see sections 4.2.1.4., 4.3.2.2., 4.7.2.1., and 4.7.2.2.

4.1.2.2. Command future indicative. The normal way to give a command in English is with the imperative mood: "Run into the forest." The same command can be given using the future indicative: "You will run into the forest." The same is true in Greek. (See section 3.4.2.2. for a further discussion.) The second English rendering suggested below is meant to leave no doubt that a command is involved. This may not be clear in versions that use the English future indicative form for the command future, so it must be pointed out in a sermon. (In the Old Testament, the Ten Commandments followed the Hebrew equivalent of the command future indicative.)

ἀγαπήσεις κύριον θεὸν σου ἐξ ὅλης τῆς καρδίας σου.

You shall love the Lord your God with all your heart (Mark 12:30).

BETTER: **Love** the Lord your God with all your heart.

4.1.2.3. Conditional indicative. The "if . . . then" pattern is commonly found in both Greek and English. These are referred to as conditional sentences. When English speakers hear *if*, they think, maybe, maybe not. Greek speakers were able to be more precise.

When Greek speakers or writers wanted to assume a condition was true for the sake of argument, they used an indicative verb in the *if* part of the sentence (the **protasis**). Also, they usually used the Greek word εἰ for *if*. Traditionally this has been called the first class conditional. In such cases, it can be better to use the word *since* or *assuming* rather than *if* in translation, or at least allude to this during the sermon.

εἰ υἱὸς **εἶ** τοῦ θεοῦ, βάλε σεαυτὸν **ἐντεῦθεν** κάτω.

Since you **are** God's Son, throw yourself down from here
(Luke 4:9).

εἰ γὰρ Ἀβραὰμ ἐξ ἔργων **ἐδικαιώθη**, ἔχει καύχημα.

For assuming Abraham **was justified** by works,
he had a ground for boasting (Rom. 4:2).

Notice that in the first example, the assumption is correct: Jesus is God's Son. In the second, the assumption is incorrect: Abraham was justified by something other than works. However, the conclusion in both cases was reached by assuming the condition to be true: Jesus was asked to throw himself down because He was God's Son; Abraham had a reason to boast if indeed he was justified by works.

When speakers wanted to assume a condition was false, for the sake of argument, they also used an indicative verb in the **protasis** in a past tense only, along with the Greek word εἰ for *if*. They also used the untranslatable word ἄν in the **apodosis**, the "then" part of the sentence, using a past tense verb. This form has been designated the second class conditional. In English, there is no way to say this except by "if . . . then." An explanation in the sermon may help.

εἰ ἦς ὧδε οὐκ ἂν ἀπέθανεν ὁ ἀδελφός μου.

If you **had been** here, my brother would not have died (John 11:21).

εἰ δὲ ἑαυτοὺς **διεκρίνομεν** οὐκ ἂν ἐκρινόμεθα.

If we **judged** ourselves, we would not be judged (1 Cor. 11:31).

In the first example, the clear implication is, "If you had been here but you weren't." Likewise, in the second instance the sense is, "If we Christians would only judge ourselves, but obviously you Corinthians haven't" (as the context makes clear).

4.1.3. Summary of the Indicative

As we have seen, most indicative forms are not worth special mention in a sermon.

1. The statement indicative and interrogative indicative are used like their English equivalents.

2. When a command future indicative is used, today's audience may need help to see that a command rather than a prediction is involved. Current English usage is unclear about this.

3. The indicative could be used in the apodosis in one of two situations. Neither of these corresponds to English. First class conditionals assumed the condition to be true for the sake of the argument. Second class conditionals assumed the condition to be false. These may call for comment in preaching or teaching.

4.2. Subjunctive Mood

The Greek subjunctive is typically used when the action of the verb is uncertain or merely potential in one way or another. This tentativeness is expressed in two distinct ways. First, subjunctives sometimes function as the main verb in a sentence. More often, subjunctives are used as a dependent verb in a clause, describing some relationship to a main verb. The Greek New Testament uses the subjunctive in only two tenses: (1) the present describes a potential action that continues, and (2) the aorist tense describes potential action.

4.2.1. Subjunctive as a Main Verb

Subjunctive main verbs are often translated with *may* or *might* as in, "I might sing."

4.2.1.1. Exhortation subjunctive. When I want someone to join me in an action, I use the English form, "Let us [ask]." In Greek this is accomplished by using a subjunctive first person plural form. Some grammarians call this the hortatory subjunctive or the cohortative subjunctive.

φάγωμεν καὶ **πίωμεν**, αὔριον γὰρ ἀποθνήσκομεν.

Let us eat and **drink,** for tomorrow we die (1 Cor. 15:32).

This can also be rendered, "We should eat . . . ," but the sense of exhortation is stronger the other way. Many examples of this use are found in the New Testament. For use in sermons, a good translation is usually enough.

4.2.1.2. Prohibition subjunctive. When second person aorist subjuntives are preceded by the negative μή, the action is conceived as a negative imperative. The action is prohibited from ever happening. Section 3.1.3. on the aorist tense also discusses this matter.

μὴ **μοιχεύσῃς**, μὴ **φονεύσῃς**.

Don't **ever commit adultery**; don't **ever murder** (Luke 18:20).

Another way to understand this is with the translation, "Don't begin to [ask]." It means to stop in advance a possible course of action. Since English versions do not convey the sense of this, it can help to mention the exact force of a prohibition subjunctive when preaching or teaching.

4.2.1.3. Denial subjunctive. Some grammarians call this the subjunctive of emphatic negation. When speakers wanted to assert as strongly as possible that an action could never ever happen, they used the denial subjunctive. It is formed by οὐ μή plus an aorist subjunctive. When preaching from a text that makes a promise applying to today's believers (as in the example following), it is worthwhile to point out the force of the denial subjunctive.

τῶν ἁμαρτιῶν αὐτῶν οὐ μὴ **μνησθῶ** ἔτι.

Their sins I **will** never any more **remember** (Heb. 8:12).

4.2.1.4. Deliberation subjunctive. When Greek speakers asked a question out of perplexity or hesitancy about the future, they used the subjunctive. This contrasts with the interrogative indicative (section 4.1.2.1.), in which the speaker was asking for facts. Sometimes the deliberation subjunctive is found with rhetorical questions, that is, questions for which the speaker already knows the answer or is about to respond.

τί **ποιήσωμεν** τοῖς ἀνθρώποις τούτοις;

What **should we do** to these men? (Acts 4:16).

πῶς δὲ **ἀκούσωσιν** χωρὶς κηρυξσσοντος;

But how **can they hear** without preaching? (Rom. 10:14).

In the first example, the answer is not known. The speakers are in a dilemma. In the second, Paul answers his rhetorical question in the following discussion. Since deliberative questions are usually translated correctly, sermonic mention is not often required.

4.2.2. Subjunctive as a Dependent Verb

The subjunctive is found much more frequently in the Greek Testament as a dependent verb than as a main verb. Five distinct functions are found in the New Testament.

4.2.2.1. Purpose subjunctive. As soon as you learned about subjunctives, you learned to use the Greek ἵνα. This Greek conjunction often introduces a subjunctive, telling the purpose of an action. The conjunction ὅπως also introduces purpose statements. Some grammars refer to these as final subjunctives. The English idea *in order that* or *so that* is a good way to interpret purpose.

πάντα ὑπομένω. . . ἵνα καὶ αὐτοὶ σωτηρίας **τύχωσιν**.

I endure everything. . . in order that they also **may obtain** salvation (2 Tim. 2:10).

ἐπιθέντα αὐτῷ τὰς χεῖρας ὅπως **ἀναβλέψῃ**.

Laying hands on him so that **he should see** (Acts 9:12).

4.2.2.2. Result subjunctive. Result is closely related to purpose. We hope that our purposes will have the result we intended. Sometimes it is hard to distinguish between the two. There are clear examples, however, of subjunctive following ἵνα meaning *so that*. Some grammars call these consecutive subjunctives.

πιστός ἐστιν καὶ δίκαιος, ἵνα **ἀφῇ** ἡμῖν τὰς ἁμαρτίας.

He is faithful and just, so that **he forgives** our sins (1 John 1:9).

In this example, clearly God's forgiveness is meant to be understood as a consequence—not the purpose—of His character. When it is difficult to decide between purpose and result, I usually decide in favor of purpose. You will usually want to note in preaching when a clause indicates purpose or result. Sometimes this will have a major impact on your sermon structure.

4.2.2.3. Content subjunctive. The Greek ἵνα was used in a variety of situations. Sometimes it introduces the content of what is wished or thought. Following ἵνα may also be found the gist of a command. Alternately, content subjunctives may express indirectly the words of a speaker and are called indirect quotation subjunctives. They may be paraphrased as a speaker's direct words.

πληρώσατέ μου τὴν χαρὰν ἵνα τὸ αὐτὸ **φρονῆτε**.

Fulfill my joy by **your thinking** the same thing (Phil. 2:2).

οὐκ ἐρωτῶ ἵνα **ἄρῃς** αὐτοὺς ἐκ τοῦ κόσμου.

I do not ask that you **take** them out of the world (John 17:15).

DIRECT: I do not ask you, "**Take** them out of the world."

In the first example, the material following ἵνα expresses the specific content of fulfilled joy. In the second example, the words of the request follow the ἵνα. Ὅτι followed by an indicative verb expresses both content and **indirect quotation**. Neither **content subjunctives** with ἵνα nor content indicatives with ὅτι call for sermonic mention.

4.2.2.4. Conditional subjunctive. We have already noted the conditional indicative (section 4.1.2.3). Greek reserved the subjunctive mood for the "maybe, maybe not" condition. This is the traditional third class conditional (see also 4.7.1.3). When the "if" part of a condition could happen either way, the condition is introduced with ἐάν, followed by a subjunctive.

ἐὰν **γήμῃ** ἡ παρθένος, οὐχ ἥμαρτεν.

If a virgin **marries**, she has not sinned (1 Cor. 7:28).

Many instances of this kind of conditional are found in the Greek Testament. In the example, sometimes the girl will marry; sometimes she will not. Because this corresponds well with English usage, it does not call for sermonic mention.

4.2.2.5. Indefinite subjunctive. A number of English terms use the -ever ending to indicate indefiniteness: *whoever, whatever, wherever, whenever,* etc. For Greek speakers, such situations of indefiniteness called for the subjunctive, often following a form of the untranslatable word ἄν.

ὃς ἂν **ἐπικαλέσηται** τὸ ὄνομα κυρίου σωθήσεται.

PERSON: Whoever **calls on** the Lord's name will be saved (Rom. 10:10).

ὅπου ἐὰν **εἰσέλθῃ** εἴπατε τῷ οἰκοδεσπότῃ.

PLACE: Wherever **he enters**, say to the owner (Mark 14:14).

ὅσα ἂν **αἰτήσῃ** τὸν θεὸν δώσει σοι ὁ θεός.

THING: God will give you whatever **you ask** from God (John 11:22).

ὅταν γάρ **ἀσθενῶ**, τότε δυνατός εἰμι.

TIME: For whenever **I am weak**, then I am strong (2 Cor 12:10).

English translations are not always careful to include the *-ever* in rendering these. Most English speakers do not pick up such a subtle difference anyway. (Leave out the *-ever* in the translations given above. Do you discern a distinction?) Such fine points are beyond the needs of most congregations.

4.2.3. Summary of the Subjunctive

1. When the subjunctive is used as a main verb, it indicates exhortation, prohibition, denial, or deliberation. Only the prohibition and denial subjunctives are worth mentioning often in sermons.

2. When subjunctive verbs are dependent, they indicate purpose, result, content, condition, or some indefinite relationship. Only purpose or result clauses need frequent mention in sermons.

4.3. Optative Mood

The optative had faded from ordinary speech so much in the first century that fewer than seventy instances occur in the entire Greek Testament. Like the subjunctive, only present and aorist forms are found. As a mood, the optative is best understood as expressing a wish on behalf of a speaker or writer.

4.3.1. Ordinary Use of the Optative

More than half the optative forms of the Greek Testament are called the **volitional optative**, that is, they express the wish, hope, or prayer of the speaker or writer.

ἔλεος ὑμῖν καὶ εἰρήνη καὶ ἀγάπη **πληθυνθείη**.

Mercy, peace, and love **be multiplied** to you (Jude 2).

ἐμοὶ δὲ μὴ **γένοιτο** καυχᾶσθαι εἰ μὴ ἐν τῷ σταυρῷ.

May it never **be** for me to boast except in the cross (Gal. 6:14).

Several translation possibilities exist for these. The first example could be rendered, "I wish that mercy, peace, and love" or, "I pray that" or "I hope that." The second example is one of the fifteen times in the New Testament that μὴ γένοιτο is found. The *King James Version* paraphrases this "God forbid." Other possibilities are "by no means," "may it not be so," or "let it never happen." For sermonic purposes the key is to translate carefully rather than to comment on the optative.

4.3.2. Special Usages of the Optative

Two specialized uses of the optative may be identified. Each of these carries the wish idea, although more indirectly.

4.3.2.1. Curse optative. In Greek the optative was used to wish harm on someone or something. Some have called this the optative of imprecation. In preaching, this calls for careful translation.

τὸ ἀργύριόν σου σὺν σοὶ **εἴη** εἰς ἀπώλειαν.

LITERAL: **May** your money with you **be** for destruction
(Acts 8.20).
BETTER: Your money perish with you!

4.3.2.2. Deliberation optative. Speakers could use either this or the deliberation subjunctive (4.2.1.4.). Deliberative optative is also used when a speaker has a question but does not have in mind a clear sense of what the answer might be. In preaching, careful translation is sufficient.

τὶ ἂν **θέλοι** ὁ σπερμολόγος οὗτος λέγειν;

Whatever **could** this babbler **wish** to say? (Acts 17:18).

4.3.3. Summary of the Optative

The optative is so rare that you seldom encounter it when preparing sermons. Remember that the optative expresses a wish. Be sure your translation is carefully done. In preaching simply refer to your translation rather than mentioning the optative by name.

4.4. Imperative Mood

The imperative, of the true moods, is the one farthest removed from reality. The indicative generally expresses action as real; the subjunctive expresses possible action; the optative expresses a wish. The imperative relates action possible only if one person's will prevails over another's. The imperative is the mood of intention. Like the subjunctive and optative, only aorist and present tense forms of the imperative are found in the Greek Testament. In the following examples I have translated the present imperatives to suggest continuing action.

4.4.1. Main Usage of the Imperative

As you might guess, the normal use of this mood is the **command imperative.** When kings spoke to subjects, masters to servants, or parents to children, the imperative was normal. We expect to find the imperative any time a superior addressed an inferior or when one with recognized authority spoke.

φεύγετε τὴν πορνείαν.

Keep fleeing immorality (1 Cor. 6:18).

τὰ τέκνα, **ὑπακούετε** τοῖς γονεῦσιν ὑμῶν.

Children, **keep obeying** your parents (Eph. 6:1).

Examples of this use abound. For preaching purposes, it is usually enough to note the command nature of the sentence. In situations involving present imperatives, use your own judgment in noting the implication of continuing action.

4.4.2. Special Uses of the Imperative

The Greek imperative is not limited to positive commands. Be alert for four specialized uses.

4.4.2.1. Prohibition imperative. A negative command is sometimes expressed by μή followed by a present imperative. In such instances, an action already under way must be stopped, although sometimes common sense indicates that this implication is too subtle. Note that this differs from the **prohibition subjunctive** (4.2.1.3).

μὴ **γογγύζετε** μετ᾽ ἀλλήλων.

Stop **grumbling** with one another (John 6:43).

μὴ **ἐρεθίζετε** τὰ τέκνα ὑμῶν.

Stop **vexing** your children (Col. 3:21).

PREFERABLE: Don't **vex** your children.

In the first example, context indicates that grumbling was already under way. It must stop. In the second instance, we should not infer that all the fathers of Colossae were vexing their children. The point of the present tense is simply, If you are vexing them, stop it immediately. The preferred translation is more generally applicable for this negative command. The guideline for recognizing this kind of imperative is to note whether μή preceeds a present imperative. When the implication is to stop doing an action, this is worth sermonic attention.

4.4.2.2. Permission imperative. Do you remember that Greek has a third person imperative that English does not have? This was a way of requesting a course of action for someone not actually present. One way to accommodate this is with the translation device "let him [ask]" or "let them [ask]." A stronger translation is often possible.

ζητησάτω εἰρήνην καὶ **διωξάτω** αὐτήν.

Let him seek peace and **let him pursue** it (1 Pet. 3:12).

ALTERNATIVE: He **must seek** peace and **must pursue** it.

μανθανέτωσαν δὲ καὶ οἱ ἡμέτεροι καλῶν ἔργων προΐστασθαι.

But also **let** our people **keep learning** to do good works (Tit. 3:14).

ALTERNATIVE: Our people **are to learn** to do good works.

The guideline for recognizing this kind of imperative is to note the third person. In a sermon perhaps the best approach is to offer two translation possibilities.

4.4.2.3. Request imperative. Sometimes second person imperatives are used when one equal speaks to another or when an inferior speaks to a superior. In such cases common sense requires that we understand a request rather than a command. Some grammars call this the imperative of entreaty. When one of my students says to me, "Give me an extension on my term paper," I recognize a plea. The word *please* is implied even if it is not used. Similarly, prayers in the New Testament often have imperative verbs, yet we understand them as humble requests rather than as commands.

ποίησόν με ὡς ἕνα τῶν μισθίων σου.

Make me as one of your hired hands [please] (Luke 15:19).

καὶ **ἄφες** ὑμῖν τὰς ἁμαρτίας.

And [please] **forgive** us our sins (Luke 11:4).

The guideline for recognizing the request imperative is to ask whether an equal or superior is addressed and to ask whether the word *please* is implied. Special sermonic attention is not usually required.

4.4.2.4. Conditional imperative. Both English and Greek use the formula IMPERATIVE + AND/KAI + FUTURE INDICATIVE to mean "if . . . then." Consider the following: "Study hard and you'll pass the exam." Clearly the meaning is, If you study hard, then you'll pass the exam.

μόνον **πίστευσον**, καὶ σωθήσεται.

GOOD: Only **believe**, and she will be saved (Luke 8:50).

BETTER: If only **you believe**, then she will be saved.

ζητεῖτε, καὶ εὑρήσετε.

GOOD: **Keep seeking**, and you will find (Luke 11:9).

BETTER: If **you keep seeking**, then you will find.

Notice that the indicative verbs following the imperative are in the future tense, which is usual for a conditional imperative. The guideline for recognizing this kind of imperative is to discover whether the formula IMPERATIVE + KAI + FUTURE INDICATIVE points to an "if . . . then" meaning. In a sermon, it may be helpful to suggest the "if . . . then" understanding, since English versions do not usually adopt this "better" rendering.

4.4.3. Summary of the Imperative

In most ways the Greek imperative parallels the English imperative.

1. The command imperative is, naturally, the main sense of the imperative.

2. The Greek prohibition imperative often carries a sense of ceasing an action—an idea that is missing from English.

3. The permission imperative has no English parallel, because English lacks a third person imperative.

4. The request imperative is a common-sense category based on the observation that imperatives do not always imply a command. Sometimes they represent an entreaty.

5. Conditional imperatives are an alternative way to make an "if . . . then" statement.

The two "near moods" are called this because none of their forms have personal endings. However, they have tense and voice, so students of Greek should study them along with the true moods.

4.5. The Infinitive

The Greek infinitive is a hybrid. It is part verb and part noun. Since about one in every sixty words of the Greek Testament is an infinitive, the infinitive cannot be ignored. As you will see in the translations, Greek infinitives cannot always be translated as English infinitives. Three tenses of Greek infinitives appear often: aorist, present, and perfect. Future infinitives are found five times in Acts and Hebrews.

4.5.1. Infinitive as a Noun

Because infinitives are partly nouns, they fit into any part of a Greek sentence that an ordinary noun could fit (for example, subject, direct object). This is called the substantive use of the infinitive. English has clear parallels: "To swim again felt good to Sue."

In this sentence the infinitive is obviously the subject. For preaching purposes, this need not be mentioned.

ἐμοὶ γὰρ τὸ **ζῆν** Χριστὸς καὶ τὸ **ἀποθανεῖν** κέρδος.

For to me **to live** is Christ and **to die** is gain (Phil. 1:21).

4.5.2. Infinitive as a Noun or Adjective Complement

In English, nouns sometimes need an infinitive to complete their meaning: "The king has the power to judge." A parallel in Greek can be found with nouns of authority, need, or fitness, and occasionally with other nouns.

ἔδωκεν αὐτοῖς ἐξουσίαν τέκνα θεοῦ **γενέσθαι**.

He gave them authority **to become** God's children (John 1:12).

Some adjectives also need an infinitive: "The king is able to judge." In Greek, adjectives reflecting ideas such as worthy, able, or full may have an infinitive to complete the meaning.

ἐγὼ τίς ἤμην δυνατὸς **κωλῦσαι** τὸν θεόν;

Who was I to be able **to oppose** God? (Acts 11:17).

Neither of these constructions offers difficulty in translation or in understanding. Sermonic attention is not required.

4.5.3. Infinitive in a Verb Phrase

Infinitives complete some English verbs: "The students are beginning to study." Greek had a parallel situation. These verbs often have an infinitive to complement them.

ἄρχομαι I begin	δεῖ it is necessary	δύναμαι I can
ἔξεστι it is lawful	ζητέω I seek	θέλω I wish
μέλλω I am about to	ὀφείλω I ought	πρέπει it is proper

οὐδεὶς δύναται δυσὶ κυρίοις **δουλεύειν**.

Nobody can **serve** two masters (Matt. 6:24).

ἀρχόμεθα πάλιν ἑαυτοὺς **συνιστάνειν**;

Are we beginning **to commend** ourselves again? (2 Cor. 3:1).

In the first example, the English *to* must be dropped following *can* for the sake of smooth translation. The same is true following *must* or *should*.

In almost all situations of infinitives as verbal complement, the main focus is on the idea contained in the infinitive rather than on the idea of the indicative verb. The key for recognizing these is to be acquainted with the list of Greek verbs that can take an infinitive complement.

A special subcategory of this is the **indirect quotation** infinitive. As in English, in Greek a speaker's words may be related indirectly by using an infinitive following another verb form: "Andy told Tina **to shut** the door." In such a situation, the direct quotation can be reconstructed easily: "Andy told Tina, 'Shut the door.'"

ὁ λέγων ἐν αὐτῷ **μένειν** ὀφείλει.

He who claims **to abide** in him ought (1 John 2:6).

DIRECT: He who says, "**I abide** in him," ought.

When dealing with an indirect quotation infinitive in a sermon, you may want to offer the direct discourse equivalent for the sake of interest or clarification.

4.5.4. Infinitive as an Adverb

For purposes of preaching, the infinitive as adverb is likely to be more important than any of the categories listed so far. In all the categories that follow, the infinitive modifies a main verb, indicating purpose, result, cause, or time of another action.

4.5.4.1. Purpose infinitive. In section 4.2.2.1, we learned about the purpose subjunctive, following ἵνα or ὅπως. The purpose infinitive, also called the final infinitive, is also used. Sometimes this is formed by the simple infinitive. In other situations the purpose infinitive follows εἰς, πρός, ὥστε, ὡς, or τοῦ. The English equivalent is often expressed as "in order to" or "for the purpose of."

καὶ εἰσῆλθεν τοῦ **μεῖναι** σὺν αὐτοῖς.

And he went in **in order to stay** with them (Luke 24:29).

And he went in **for the purpose of staying** with them.

μὴ γὰρ οἰκίας οὐκ ἔχετε εἰς τὸ **ἐσθίειν** καὶ **πίνειν**;

Don't you have houses **to eat** and **drink** in? (1 Cor. 11:22).

Don't you have houses **for the purpose of eating** and **drinking**?

Many times such purpose clauses need sermonic attention.

4.5.4.2. Result infinitive. Section 4.2.2.2. introduced the result subjunctive (following ἵνα). The result infinitive in Greek, also called the consecutive infinitive, is found most plainly following ὥστε. Sometimes it is made by the simple infinitive; occasionally it follows εἰς or τοῦ. A frequent English translation is "so that" or "resulting in." Sometimes distinguishing precisely between purpose and result is difficult.

καὶ ἐὰν ἔχω πᾶσαν τὴν πίστιν ὥστε ὄρη **μεθιστάναι**.

And if I have all faith **so that I move** mountains (1 Cor. 13:2).

And if I have all faith **resulting in my moving** mountains.

αὐτὸς τὸ πρόσωπον ἐστήρισεν τοῦ **πορεύεσθαι** εἰς Ἰερουσαλήμ.

He set his face **so that he went** to Jerusalem (Luke 9:51).

He set his face **resulting in going** to Jerusalem.

The second example illustrates the difficulty of determining precisely between result and purpose. The text may be better read, "He set his face **in order that** he should go to Jerusalem." In any event, in this instance the intended purpose had its desired result. It is best not to labor such ambiguities. They do not always have to be decided.

4.5.4.3. Causal infinitive. Because English has no causal infinitive, the Greek causal infinitive is not translated with the English infinitive (for example, to ask). The Greeks often used the formula διὰ τό + INFINITIVE to show cause. They also used ὅτι + INDICATIVE. The διὰ τό could also be omitted. Often reference to this adverbial sense fits into a sermon.

οὐκ ἔχετε διὰ τὸ μὴ **αἰτεῖσθαι** ὑμᾶς.

You do not have because you **do** not **ask** (Jas. 4:2).

οὐκ ἔσχηκα ἄνεσιν τῷ πνεύματί μου τῷ μὴ **εὑρεῖν** με Τίτον.

I had no rest in my spirit because I **did** not **find** Titus (2 Cor. 2:13).

The second example also illustrates the unexpected use of an accusative noun or pronoun (με) to indicate the **subject of an infinitive**, rather than the expected nominative. Some grammars call this the **accusative of general reference**. These do not call for special exegetical attention; however, they will confuse you as you work with the text unless you are aware of them.

4.5.4.4. Time infinitive. English has no temporal infinitive, so the translation "to [ask]" is not used. Three time relationships are possible with reference to a main verb: before, while, and after. Greek infinitives express each of these notions when prefaced by the right formula.

To express *before*, the words πρὸ τοῦ or πρὶν (ἤ) go before the infinitive. This is called **antecedent action** to the main verb.

πρὸ τοῦ δὲ **ἐλθεῖν** τὴν πίστιν ὑπὸ νόμον ἐφρουρούμεθα.

Before faith **came** we were imprisoned by law (Gal. 3:21).

πρὶν ἀλέκτορα **φωνῆσαι** δὶς τρίς με ἀπαρνήσῃ.

Before a cock **crows** twice, you'll deny me three times (Mark 14:72).

To express *while*, the words ἐν τῷ go before the infinitive. This is simultaneous or contemporaneous action to the main verb.

ἐν τῷ **καθεύδειν** τοὺς ἀνθρώπους ἦλθεν αὐτοῦ ὁ ἐχθρός.

While people **were sleeping** his enemy came (Matt. 13:25).

To express *after*, the words μετὰ τὸ go in front of the infinitive. This is called subsequent action to the main verb.

συνεπίομεν αὐτῷ μετὰ τὸ **ἀναστῆναι** αὐτόν.

We drank with him after he **arose** (Acts 10:41).

These four examples also illustrate the use of the accusative as the subject of the infinitive (see 4.5.4.3.). Time infinitives call for care in translation, but sermonic comment is not necessary.

4.5.4.5. Independent infinitive. Occasionally Greek infinitives go their own way. They could be used when an imperative was expected or in some other unusual way. This category accounts for infinitives that fit nowhere else.

κλαίειν μετὰ κλαιόντων.

Weep with those who weep (Rom. 12:15).

4.5.5. Summary of the Infinitive

Infinitives were used more broadly in Greek than in English. Most of the time, the best way to deal with infinitives is to be sure you understand how to translate them.

1. The infinitive used as a noun element or substantive is much like English usage. The "to" translation is adequate.

2. The same may be said of the infinitive as a complement (modifier) of a noun or adjective. The "to" translation is adequate.

3. Greek and English share the use of an infinitive in a verb phrase. Sometimes the "to" drops out in English translation.

4. The adverbial infinitive of purpose and result deserves careful consideration, both in sermon preparation and often in the pulpit. Distinguish between these notions when you are able to do so.

5. The causal infinitive has no English parallel. Careful translation includes "because." A sermonic subpoint may be based on observing this distinction.

6. Time infinitives also have no English parallel. As long as these are translated into good English, they do not require mention in preaching.

7. Independent infinitives are rare and include a variety of situations that you will recognize during your study of the text. Call attention to these only if you feel it absolutely necessary.

4.6. The Participle

In elementary Greek classes, studying the participle is the most dreaded part of the task. Greek participles have so many different forms (that is, **syntactical words**, see 1.1.1) because they are similar to adjectives. Like other Greek adjectives, participles had gender, case, and number. Just like all Greek verbs, they had to have tense and voice. In the New Testament, aorist, present, and perfect participles abound, accounting for about five percent of the total word count. A handful of future participles is also in the New Testament.

4.6.1. Participle as Adjective

Since participles are all verbal adjectives, they sometimes function as ordinary adjectives, that is, they modify or describe a noun. Sometimes this is called the **attributive participle**.

ὁ ἀντίδικος ὑμῶν διάβολος ὡς λέων **ὠρυόμενος** περιπατεῖ.

Your enemy the devil walks as a **roaring** lion (1 Pet 5:8).

ἡ εἰρήνη τοῦ θεοῦ ἡ **ὑπερέχουσα** πάντα νοῦν.

God's peace that **surpasses** all understanding (Phil. 4:7).

A special subcategory of this is the **object complement** participle. This occurs when the main verb deals with perception (for example, seeing, hearing). The participle describes an action being performed by the direct object (and perceived by the subject). (Do not confuse this with the verb phrase participle, explained in section 4.6.4.)

Ἰησοῦς οὖν εἶδεν αὐτὴν **κλαίουσαν**.

Therefore Jesus saw her **weeping** (John 11:33).

Another subcategory is the **subject complement** or **predicate adjective**. This occurs when the main verb is a form of εἰμί and the participle describes the subject. (Do not confuse this with the **peri-**

phrastic, in which two verb forms, εἰμί plus a participle, combine as if they were a single verb. See 4.6.4. for this usage.)

ἤμην δὲ **ἀγνοούμενος** τῷ προσώπῳ ταῖς ἐκκλησίαις.

But I was **unknown** by face to the churches (Gal. 1:22).

All adjective participles may be dealt with in the sermon preparation process. They do not require public attention.

4.6.2. Participle as a Noun

When you first learned about Greek adjectives, you learned that they could serve as nouns. For example, if ὁ πιστὸς ἀπόστολος means the faithful apostle, then ὁ πιστός can mean the faithful one. Thus, if ὁ βλέπων ἀπόστολος means the seeing apostle (the apostle who sees), then ὁ βλέπων can mean the seeing one (the one who sees). When a Greek participle functions as if it were a noun, this is called the **substantive** use of the participle. As such, the participle can be a subject, an object of the preposition, or fill any other syntactical slot that an ordinary noun occupied. This is quite similar to the use of the infinitive as a noun (4.5.1). Substantive participles usually have an article attached.

τί ζητεῖτε τὸν **ζῶντα** μετὰ τῶν **νεκρῶν**;

Why do you seek the **living one** among the **dead ones**?
(Luke 24:5).

τῷ δὲ **ἐργαζομένῳ** ὁ μισθὸς οὐ λογίζεται κατὰ χάριν.

But for **one who works,** salary is not considered a gift (Rom. 4:4).

In these examples the article precedes the participles. Also, note that the English "he who [asks]," "the one who [asks]," "those who [ask]" are often used to translate these, but they are by no means the only acceptable translations. There is no reason to refer to this construction in a sermon, although you may want to offer alternative renderings.

4.6.3. Circumstantial Participle

By far the most important use of the participle for preaching purposes is the **circumstantial participle**. Some call this the adverbial participle. This occurs when the participle describes (modifies) another verb within the sentence, usually the main verb. It describes circumstances under which the action of the main verb occurred. Such participles are never preceded by an article.

Scholars have disagreed sharply concerning the precise interpretation of specific circumstantial participles. For all the following, the guideline is context and common sense. Proper English supporting terms (while, although, if, because) are necessary to clarify what is implicit in the Greek text. In the following discussion a literal translation of the participle is followed by a better English rendering with supporting terms.

4.6.3.1. Circumstantial participle of time. This is the most frequent kind of adverbial participle. When you first learned participles, perhaps you learned to translate present tense adverbial participles with *while, when,* or *as,* reserving *after* for aorist participles. Now you need to unlearn that; most but not all adverbial participles can be translated as temporal. Furthermore, some aorist participles indicate action occurring at the same time as the main verb (see 3.1.3.). Again, context and common sense must prevail.

ἐλθὼν δὲ εἰς τὴν οἰκίαν οὐκ ἀφῆκεν εἰσελθεῖν τινα.

But **entering** the house, he did not allow anyone to enter (Luke 8:51).

BETTER: But **when he entered** the house, he did not allow. . .

Clearly in this context, the relationship between entering and allowing is temporal; entering preceded allowing. None of the other circumstantial notions mentioned below fits.

4.6.3.2. Circumstantial participle of purpose. In some circumstances, a participle indicates the purpose of the action of the main verb. This is an alternative for the purpose infinitive (see 4.5.4.1). Some grammars call this the final participle. Both present and future participles are used in this way. The supporting phrase *in order to* or *in order that* is to be introduced in the English rendering.

ἀπέστειλεν αὐτὸν **εὐλογοῦντα** ὑμᾶς.

He sent him **blessing** you (Acts 3:26).

BETTER: He sent him **in order to bless** you.

4.6.3.3. Circumstantial participle of result. In a few instances participles tell the result of an action. These are an alternative to the result infinitive, called **consecutive participles** (see 4.5.4.2.). Some translation such as *so that* or *resulting in* are to be supplied.

οὐκέτι ἀφίετε αὐτὸν οὐδὲν ποιῆσαι τῷ πατρι . . .
ἀκυροῦντες τὸν λογὸν τοῦ θεοῦ.

No longer do you allow him to do anything for his father . . . **nullifying** the Word of God (Mark 7:12–13).

BETTER: No longer do you allow him to do anything for his father . . . **resulting in nullifying** the Word of God.

4.6.3.4. Circumstantial participle of cause. A participle may indicate the cause of the action of the main verb. This is a substitute for the causal infinitive (see 4.5.4.3.). This causal participle expresses the ground or basis for the action of the main verb. The supporting term *because* or *since* is used in English translation.

ἡ εὐσέβεια . . . ὠφέλιμός ἐστιν ἐπαγγελίαν **ἔχουσα** ζωῆς.

Piety is useful . . . , **having** the promise of life (1 Tim. 4:8).

BETTER: Piety is useful. . . , **since it has** the promise of life.

4.6.3.5. Circumstantial participle of condition. A participle may function as the if part of a conditional sentence. Like third class conditionals (see 4.2.2.4.), such participles state a condition to be fulfilled before the action of the main verb can happen. The supporting term *if* is required.

θερίσομεν μὴ **ἐκλυόμενοι**.

We will reap **fainting** not (Gal. 6:9).

BETTER: We will reap **if we do** not **faint**.

This example certainly could be translated as a time participle: "when we do not faint." However, in the context of Galatians 6, a good case can be made for the conditional rendering.

4.6.3.6. Circumstantial participle of concession. The notion of concession is the opposite of condition, sometimes called adversative. In this situation, the action of the main verb is accomplished in spite of the action of the participle. Adverse circumstances have not halted an outcome (or else a situation has produced an unexpected result). The supporting terms *even if, although,* or *in spite of* are required in English.

δι᾽ ὅλης νυκτὸς **κοπιάσαντες** οὐδὲν ἐλάβομεν.

Having toiled all night, we caught nothing (Luke 5:5).

BETTER: **Although we toiled** all night, we caught nothing.

4.6.3.7. Circumstantial participle of means. Participles often tell how the action of a main verb is accomplished. Some grammars call this the instrumental participle. The appropriate supporting terms in English translation are *by means of* or *by [ask]ing.*

ἑαυτὸν ἐκένωσεν μορφὴν δούλου **λαβών**.

He emptied himself, **taking** a slave's form (Phil. 2:7).

BETTER: He emptied himself **by taking** a slave's form.

This example shows that important theological issues can depend on accurate handling of circumstantial participles.

4.6.3.8. Circumstantial participle of manner. Participles sometimes answer the question how. This is close to the pure adverb idea, and is often called the **modal participle**. It is difficult to make a great distinction between means and manner. Some grammars do not distinguish between the two, so do not feel that you must always arrive at a definitive answer. Biblical writers did not consciously distinguish between the two. They just wrote using terms that were clear to them and their audiences. Supporting terms are *by [ask]ing* or *in an [ask]ing manner*. Manner participles are also often translated with the simple *[ask]ing*.

ἦλθεν ὁ Ἰησοῦς εἰς τὴν Γαλιλαίαν **κηρύσσων** τὸ εὐαγγέλιον.

Jesus came to Galilee **preaching** the gospel (Mark 1:14).

4.6.4. Verb Phrase Participle

The fourth main way in which Greek uses participles is to complete the meaning of a verb in some way other than as an adverb modifier. The participle is the second member of such a verb phrase. You need to be aware of two kinds.

First, some main verbs express a thought that is incomplete and needs a participle to fill in the meaning. This is similar to the verb complement infinitive (see 4.5.3.). In English, for example, we can say "They began studying" just as easily as "They began to study." Verbs of perception, emotion, knowing, beginning, and ending may have such a participle. In these instances, the action of the participle is more important than the action of the main verb. A good way to identify these participles is to note that they answer the question what.

ἐτέλεσεν ὁ Ἰησοῦς **διατάσσων** τοῖς δώδεκα μαθηταῖς.

Jesus finished **instructing** the twelve disciples (Matt. 11:1).

The second kind of verb phrase participle is the **periphrastic**. This is the use of two verb forms (a helping verb and a main verb) when one word could have been used, as in the English, "she is studying" instead of "she studies." These are made by a participle following a form of εἰμί. Chapter 3 includes discussion of periphrastics for the present, the perfect, the future, the imperfect, and the pluperfect (see 3.2.1., 3.3.1., 3.4., 3.5., and 3.6.).

τῇ γὰρ χάριτί **ἐστε σεσῳσμένοι** διὰ πίστεως.

For by grace **you have been saved** through faith (Eph. 2:8).

This is a perpiphrastic because the two verb forms ἐστε σεσῳσμένοι could have been rendered as a single perfect passive verb form σέσωσθε. Periphrastics are a matter of style and preference by individual Greek writers. All the kinds of participles mentioned in section 4.6.4. should be dealt with in sermon preparation, so that there is no need to mention them in the sermon.

4.6.5. Independent Participle

At times Greek participles function as main verbs, either indicatives or imperatives. Grammarians refer to these as participles of attendant circumstance, participles of coordinate circumstance, or unrestricted participles. Sometimes a participle is parallel to a main verb, supplying information as important as the main verb. Usually these precede the main verb. They are translated as an English main verb followed by a supplied *and*.

Ἰωάννης . . . **πέμψας** διὰ τῶν μαθητῶν αὐτοῦ εἶπεν αὐτῷ.

John. . . **sent** through his disciples **and** said to him (Matt. 11:2–3).

Μάρκον **ἀναλαβὼν** ἄγε μετὰ σεαυτοῦ.

Fetch Mark **and** bring him with you (2 Tim. 4:11).

In the first example, the participle functions as an indicative statement; in the second it works as an imperative. Another example of the independent imperative participle is the Great Commission text, Matthew 28:19–20. Occasionally participles function as independent imperatives without a main verb.

οἱ οἰκέται **ὑποτασσόμενοι** ἐν παντὶ φόβῳ τοῖς δεσπόταις.

Slaves, **submit** with all respect to your masters (1 Pet. 2:18).

4.6.6. Summary of the Participle

1. If adjective participles are translated accurately, they require no special mention.
2. The same can be said of participles used as substantives.
3. When participles describe circumstances under which another (main) verbal action occurred, carefully search for the precise sense implied by the context. Some kind of time relationship is almost always involved. However, seven other circumstances are possible. You may want to consult several translations and commentaries, but these do not always agree on these matters. If you are reasonably confident of the circumstance indicated by the participle, you will want to bring this out in your preaching. Do not forget, however, that there were other, less ambiguous ways that a Greek writer could indicate such circumstances.
4. As in English, participles function in verb phrases in several different ways. The periphrastic is especially common. Such participles are best dealt with in translation rather than by specific discussion in the pulpit.

5. The participle as an independent verb can ordinarily be dealt with by careful translation, except when the participle carries imperative force.

4.7. Supplement: Formal Conditions, Negatives, and Quotations

4.7.1. Formal Conditions

In classical Greek four distinct formulas were used to express "if. . .then" sentences, all depending on the nature of the condition expressed. By the time the New Testament was written, the boundaries between the formal classes of conditions were blurring. As always, you must use your common sense when interpreting a conditional sentence. In general, however, the classical formulas (except for the fourth class) are found in every part of the New Testament.

Occasionally, the conditions are mixed (as in Luke 17:6 and Acts 24:19). In such instances common sense must prevail.

4.7.1.1. Condition assumed true. This is the traditional first class condition (4.1.2.3.). If a speaker or writer wanted to assume that a condition was true for the sake of argument—whether in fact it *was* true—he used a first class condition. Because the condition was thought of as true, an indicative verb was used in the *if* part (protasis) of the sentence. The *then* part (apodosis) of the sentence could use indicative, subjunctive or imperative verbs. The proper word for *if* was εἰ; occasionally ἐάν was used. Whenever the context indicates that the condition was in fact true, εἰ can be translated *since* or *because*.

εἰ ζῶμεν πνεύματι, πνεύματι καὶ στοιχῶμεν.

GOOD: **If we live by the Spirit**, let's also walk by the Spirit (Gal. 5:25).

BETTER: **Since we live by the Spirit** . . .

In this example, Paul is assuming that both he and his readers live by the Spirit. The exhortation is based on the common Christian experience of living by the Spirit.

4.7.1.2. Condition assumed false. This is the traditional second class condition (see 3.5.2.2. and 4.1.2.3.). When a speaker or writer wanted to emphasize that a condition was false or unreal, he used a second class condition. The standard word for *if* was εἰ, and the verb was limited to a past tense of the indicative mood. The apodosis used the untranslatable word ἄν and a past tense of the indicative mood. The apodasis in second class conditional sentences showed what would have been true if only the protasis had been true. In English translation, the word *would* is always needed.

εἰ γὰρ ἡ πρώτη ἐκείνη ἦν ἄμεμπτος, οὐκ ἂν δευτέρας ἐζητεῖτο τόπος.

For if the first [covenant] had been blameless,
place for a second would not have been sought (Heb. 8:7).

The logical point being made by the author of Hebrews is that something was defective with the first covenant. If the first covenant had proven to be blameless, the second covenant would never have been made.

4.7.1.3. True condition. This is the third class condition (see 4.2.2.4). This formula was used when the condition could go either way in the mind of the speaker or writer. The usual word for *if* was ἐάν, and it was followed by a subjunctive verb. (The words ἄν and εἰ could also be used to express *if.*) The apodosis usually employed the indicative or imperative, rarely the subjunctive. It shows what the result will be when the protasis is true. Look for some future implication in third class conditional sentences.

ἐὰν ἔλθω, ὑπομνήσω αὐτοῦ τὰ ἔργα ἃ ποιεῖ.

If I come I will point out his works that he is doing (3 John 10).

John seems unsure whether he will travel (see v. 14). If he does, the offender will be rebuked. If he does not, John assumes the offense will go unchecked.

4.7.2. Negatives

Greek rather carefully distinguishes between negatives using forms of οὐ and negatives using forms of μή. The following list shows the most common negative words.

οὐ (οὐκ, οὐχ)	not	μή
οὐδέ	and not, neither	μηδέ
οὐδείς	no one	μηδείς
οὐδέποτε	never	μηδέποτε
οὐδέπω	not yet	μηδέπω
οὐκέτι	no longer	μηκέτι
οὔπω	not yet	μήπω
οὔτε	and not, neither	μήτε

This list does not include any words beginning with the **alpha privative**, a prefix that functions like the English *un-* (for example ἄκαρπος, unfruitful). The easiest way to become familiar with these is to look over the words beginning with alpha in your lexicon.

4.7.2.1. Usage with forms of οὐ. In the indicative mood οὐ is the normal particle used in making negative assertions. With the future indicative, the emphatic negative combination οὐ μή is found.

οὐκ ἐψεύσω ἀνθρώποις ἀλλὰ τῷ θεῷ.

You did **not** lie to people but to God (Acts 5:1).

οἱ δὲ λόγοι μου οὐ μὴ παρελεύσονται.

But my words will **never** pass away (Luke 21:33).

Unlike English, Greek grammar uses the double and triple negatives, with either forms of οὐ or μή.

ἔθηκεν αὐτὸν ἐν μνήματι λαξευτῷ οὗ
οὐκ ἦν οὐδεὶς οὔπω κείμενος.

He placed him in a rock-hewn tomb
where **nobody** had **ever** been laid (Luke 23:53).

When a speaker asked a rhetorical question for which he expected the answer yes, οὐ was used in the question.

οὐκ εἰμὶ ἐλεύθερος; οὐκ εἰμὶ ἀπόστολος;

I am free, **am I not**? I am an apostle, **am I not**? (1 Cor. 9:1)

MORE CONCISE: Am I **not** free? Am I **not** an apostle?

In a first class condition (see 4.7.1.1), a speaker or writer could assume some negative assertions as true. In such a case, οὐ is included in the protasis.

εἴ τις ἐν λόγῳ οὐ πταίει, οὗτος τέλειος ἀνήρ.

If one does **not** offend in speech, he is a perfect man (Jas. 3:2).

4.7.2.2. Usage with forms of μή. Outside the indicative mood (that is, with subjunctives, imperatives, optatives, infinitives, and participles), μή is the normal particle used in making negative assertions. With the aorist subjunctive, the emphatic negative οὐ μή is found.

ἵνα μὴ λυπῆσθε καθὼς καὶ οἱ λοιποί.

So that you will **not** grieve as others [do] (1 Thess. 4:13).

μακάριος ἀνὴρ οὗ οὐ μὴ λογίσηται κύριος ἁμαρτίαν.

Blessed is the man against whom the
Lord **never** counts sin (Rom. 4:8).

When someone asked a rhetorical question expecting *no* for an answer, μή was used in the question, even when the main verb was indicative.

μὴ πάντες χαρίσματα ἔχουσιν ἰαμάτων;
μὴ πάντες γλώσσαις λαλοῦσιν;

Not all have gifts of healing, **do they**?

Not all speak with tongues, **do they**? (1 Cor. 12:30)

MORE CONCISE: Do all have gifts of healing?
Do all speak with tongues?

In a second class condition (see 4.7.1.2.), a speaker or writer could assume some negative assertion as untrue. In such a case μή is included in the protasis. Such a negative is called an **exception**, and the words *except* or *unless* are used in translation.

In the example that follows, the assertion "the Lord of hosts did not leave us descendants" is false from the writer's point of view. The truth is that the Lord of hosts did leave us descendants; therefore, "we did not become (destroyed) like Sodom."

Εἰ **μὴ** κύριος Σαβαὼθ ἐγκατέλιπεν ἡμῖν σπέρμα, ὡς
Σόδομα ἂν ἐγενήθημεν.

If the Lord of hosts had **not** left us descendants,
we would have become like Sodom (Rom. 9:29).

MORE CONCISE: **Unless** the Lord of hosts had left us
descendants . . .

In a third class condition (see 4.7.1.3), a speaker or writer could present a negative condition. In such a case μή was included in the protasis. This too is called an exception, with the words *except* or *unless* as useful translations. In the example that follows, the further implication is, "If you do repent, you will not perish."

ἐὰν **μὴ** μετανοῆτε πάντες ὁμοίως ἀπολεῖσθε.

If you do **not** repent, you all will perish too (Luke 13:3).

MORE CONCISE: **Unless** you repent, you all will perish too.

4.7.3. Quotations

Ancient Greek had no quotation marks, nor do most modern printed Greek Testaments. Usually, it is easy to tell what is quoted from the context. However, sometimes interpreters differ. A well-known example is John 3. Where do Jesus' words leave off and the Evangelist's comments begin? The Discourse Segmentation Apparatus of the fourth edition of the United Bible Societies' *The Greek*

New Testament documents where various Greek Testaments as well as translations have differed about this (and other matters).

In considering quotations, remember the difference between direct and indirect discourse. Only direct discourse uses the exact words of a speaker.

DIRECT: John said, "Jim closed the door."
INDIRECT: John said that Jim had closed the door.
DIRECT: John said, "Close the door, Jim."
INDIRECT: John told Jim to close the door.

4.7.3.1. Direct quotations. In Greek, direct discourse is often, but not always, introduced by ὅτι. This ὅτι is not translated. It functions as a beginning quotation mark. Many Greek Testaments mark the beginning of all direct quotations with a capital letter.

λέγουσιν αὐτῷ ὅτι Πάντες ζητουσίν σε.

They said to him, "Everyone is looking for you" (Mark 1:37).

λέγει αὐτοῖς, ῎Αγωμεν ἀλλαχοῦ.

He said to them, "Let's go elsewhere" (Mark 1:38).

4.7.3.2. Indirect quotations. As in English, Greek indirect discourse tells the content of what was spoken without quoting the speaker's exact words. Many indirect quotations in Greek begin with ὅτι, translated "that." This corresponds well to English (see the first English example in 4.7.3.). Another typical formula for indirect quotations is to use an infinitive (see the second English example in 4.7.3.). This is also similar to English.

In a few instances participle clauses are used to report indirect speech. English has no parallel usage. Occasionally ἵνα or ὅπως is used to introduce indirect discourse. We can do something similar in English.

In the following examples, I have verified that each text is an indirect quotation by recasting it as a direct citation. In your messages, you can often retell a biblical narrative vividly by recasting indirect discourse as direct quotation.

ἐὰν εἴπωμεν ὅτι ἁμαρτίαν οὐκ ἔχομεν, ἑαυτοὺς πλανῶμεν.

If we say **that we have no sin**, we deceive ourselves (1 John 1:8).

Verification: If we say, "**We have no sin**," we deceive ourselves.

Infinitive: τῷ Παύλῳ ἔλεγον . . . **μὴ ἐπιβαίνειν εἰς Ἰεροσόλυμα.**

They kept telling Paul . . . **not to go to Jerusalem** (Acts 21:4).

Verification: They kept telling Paul. . . , "**Don't go to Jerusalem.**"

Participle: ἀκούομεν γάρ **τινας περιπατοῦντας ἐν ὑμῖν ἀτάκτως**.

For we have heard **that some of you live in laziness** (2 Thess. 3:11).

Verification: For we have heard, **"Some of them live in laziness."**

Ἵνα: ἠρώτα αὐτὸν **ἵνα τὸ δαιμόνιον ἐκβάλῃ ἐκ τῆς θυγαρὸς αὐτῆς**.

She asked him **that he cast the demon from her daughter**.
(Mark 7:26).

Verification: She asked him,
"Will you cast the demon from my daughter?"

Summary of Mood Syntax

1. INDICATIVE

STATEMENT	=	main use
INTERROGATIVE	=	special use
COMMAND FUTURE	=	special use
CONDITIONAL (first class or second class)	=	special use

2. SUBJUNCTIVE

EXHORTATION (or HORTATORY or COHORATIVE)	=	main verb use
PROHIBITION (aorist tense)	=	main verb use
DENIAL (or EMPHATIC NEGATION)	=	main verb use
DELIBERATION	=	main verb use
PURPOSE (or FINAL)	=	dependent verb use
RESULT (or CONSECUTIVE)	=	dependent verb use
CONTENT (includes INDIRECT QUOTATION)	=	dependent verb use
CONDITIONAL (third class)	=	dependent verb use
INDEFINITE (-*ever* translation)	=	dependent verb use

3. OPTATIVE

VOLITIONAL	=	main use
CURSE (or IMPRECATION)	=	special use
DELIBERATION	=	special use

4. IMPERATIVE

COMMAND	=	main use
PROHIBITION (present tense)	=	special use
PERMISSION (third person)	=	special use
REQUEST (or ENTREATY)	=	special use
CONDITIONAL	=	special use

5. INFINITIVE

NOUN ELEMENT (SUBSTANTIVE)		
NOUN OR ADJECTIVE COMPLEMENT		
VERB PHRASE (includes INDIRECT QUOTATION)		
PURPOSE (or FINAL)	=	adverbial use
RESULT (or CONSECUTIVE)	=	adverbial use
CAUSE (or CAUSAL)	=	adverbial use
TIME (or TEMPORAL)	=	adverbial use
INDEPENDENT	=	unexpected use

6. PARTICIPLE

ADJECTIVE (includes SUBJECT COMPLEMENT and OBJECT COMPLEMENT)		
NOUN ELEMENT (SUBSTANTIVE)		
CIRCUMSTANTIAL (TIME, PURPOSE, RESULT, CAUSE, CONDITION, CONCESSION, MEANS, or MANNER)	=	adverbial use
VERB PHRASE (incl. PERIPHRASTIC)	=	dependent verb use
INDEPENDENT VERB (includes UNRESTRICTED)	=	main verb use

For Further Reading

Blass, F., and A. Debrunner. *A Greek Grammar of the New Testament and Other Early Christian Literature.* Trans. and rev. Robert W. Funk, 181–220. University of Chicago Press, 1961.

Brooks, James A., and Carlton L. Winbery. *Syntax of New Testament Greek,* 104–38. Washington: University Press of America, 1979.

Burton, Ernest de Witt. *Syntax of the Moods and Tenses in New Testament Greek,* 73–177. Edinburgh: T. & T. Clark, 1898.

Dana, H. E., and Julius R. Mantey. *A Manual Grammar of the Greek New Testament,* 165–76, 208–33. New York: Macmillan Co., 1927.

MacDonald, William G. *Greek Enchiridion: A Concise Handbook of Grammar for Translation and Exegesis,* 41–62. Peabody, Mass.: Hendrickson Publishers, 1986.

Moule, C. F. D. *An Idiom Book of New Testament Greek.* 2nd ed. 20–23, 99–105, 126–29. Cambridge University Press, 1959.

Moulton, James Hope. *A Grammar of New Testament Greek.* Vol. 3, *Syntax,* by Nigel Turner, 90–162. Edinburgh: T. & T. Clark, 1963.

Robertson, A. T. *A Grammar of the Greek New Testament in the Light of Historical Research,* 911–1141. Nashville: Broadman Press, 1934.

Now Let's Apply!

All verb forms from Matthew 4:1–11 and Philippians 1:3–11 are reproduced below. Tense and mood are listed beside each. Determine what the mood significance is for each one. Then write *yes* or *no* indicating whether you believe this verb form is worth mentioning in a sermon. The first two forms for each text have been completed to help get you started. Plan to spend at least half an hour working before you go to the answer key.

Matthew 4

VERB	TENSE/ MOOD	MOOD SIGNIFICANCE	SERMON MENTION?
Verse 1:			
ἀνήχθη	aorist indicative	statement	no
πειρασθῆναι	aorist infinitive	purpose	yes
Verse 2:			
νηστεύσας	aorist participle		

| ἐπείνασεν | aorist indicative | _____ | _____ |

Verse 3:

προσελθὼν	aorist participle	_____	_____
πειράζων	present participle	_____	_____
εἶπεν	aorist indicative	_____	_____
εἶ	present indicative	_____	_____
εἰπέ	aorist imperative	_____	_____
γένωνται	aorist subjunctive	_____	_____

Verse 4:

ἀποκριθείς	aorist participle	_____	_____
εἶπεν	aorist indicative	_____	_____
γέγραπται	perfect indicative	_____	_____
ζήσεται	future indicative	_____	_____
ἐκπορευομένῳ	present participle	_____	_____

Verse 5:

| παραλαμβάνει | present indicative | _____ | _____ |
| ἔστησεν | aorist ndicative | _____ | _____ |

Verse 6:

| λέγει | present indicative | _____ | _____ |
| εἶ | present indicative | _____ | _____ |

βάλε   aorist
                imperative

γέγραπται   perfect
                indicative

ἐντελεῖται   future
                indicative

ἀροῦσίν   future
                indicative

προσκόψῃς   aorist
                subjunctive

Verse 7:

ἔφη   aorist
                indicative

γέγραπται   perfect
                indicative

ἐκπειράσεις   future
                indicative

Verse 8:

παραλαμβάνει   present
                indicative

δείκνυσιν   present
                indicative

Verse 9:

εἶπεν   aorist
                indicative

δώσω   future
                indicative

πεσὼν   aorist
                participle

προσκυνήσῃς   aorist
                subjunctive

Verse 10:

λέγει   present
                indicative

ὕπαγε   present
                imperative

γέγραπται	perfect indicative		
προσκυνήσεις	future indicative		
λατρεύσεις	future indicative		
Verse 11:			
ἀφίησιν	present indicative		
προσῆλθον	aorist indicative		
διηκόνουν	aorist indicative		

After you have completed the chart on Matthew 4:1–11, look back over your work. Underline the five verb forms that you think are most interesting from the point of view of mood and that you would consider giving sermonic attention. Can you justify your choices?

Philippians 1

VERB	TENSE/ MOOD	MOOD SIGNIFICANCE	SERMON MENTION?
Verse 3:			
εὐχαριστῶ	present indicative	statement	yes
Verse 4:			
ποιούμενος	present participle	circum. (time)	no
Verse 6:			
πεποιθὼς	perfect participle		
ἐναρξάμενος	aorist participle		
ἐπιτελέσει	future indicative		

Verse 7:

ἐστιν	present indicative	_____	_____
φρονεῖν	present infinitive	_____	_____
ἔχειν	present infinitive	_____	_____
ὄντας	present participle	_____	_____

Verse 8:

| ἐπιποθῶ | present indicative | _____ | _____ |

Verse 9:

| προσεύχομαι | present indicative | _____ | _____ |
| περισσεύῃ | present subjunctive | _____ | _____ |

Verse 10:

δοκιμάζειν	present infinitive	_____	_____
διαφέροντα	present participle	_____	_____
ἦτε	present subjunctive	_____	_____

Verse 11:

| πεπληρωμένοι | perfect participle | _____ | _____ |

After you have completed the chart on Philippians 1:3–11, look back over your work. Underline the five verb forms that you think are most interesting from the point of view of mood, and that you would consider giving sermonic attention. Can you justify your choices?

Genitive
Case Forms

When you first studied Greek, you learned to render the genitive case with the translation *of.* This little English word, however, functions in a bewildering of number of ways, some of which contradict each other. Consider the fourteen instances of *of* in the following paragraph.

> Samuel Jones was born ten miles south of Dallas, a man of common farm folks. His father died of strep throat, which was stupid of him since he lost the bottle of penicillin he kept on hand. Half of the farm Samuel sold, and he spent most of his time writing stories of his hard luck. The mother of Samuel, eased of her hard life, moved off to the city of Houston. Freed from his fool of a father, he developed a love of the land. Samuel Jones later became known as a man of courage.

This paragraph could have been written as follows:

> Samuel Jones was born ten miles south measuring from Dallas, a man derived from common farm folk. His father died because of strep throat, which was stupid on his part, since he lost the bottle containing penicillin he kept on hand. Half—a portion of the entire—the farm Samuel sold, and he spent most—a portion expended from—of his time writing stories about his hard luck. The mother related to Samuel, eased from her hard life, moved off to the city one member of which class is Houston. Freed from his fool that was a father, Samuel developed a love for the land. Samuel

Jones later became known as a man characterized by courage.

Complicated, isn't it? If you consult any standard English dictionary, you will find other ways in which *of* is used. Greek genitive case forms express an even broader range of meanings than the English *of.* The genitive warrants the most careful attention of all Greek cases.

Before we look at the ways the Greek genitive is used, I must mention the ablative. Greek grammarians following A. T. Robertson have used an eight-case system in which the ablative and genitive were considered two separate cases. However, most contemporary Greek scholars, and almost all Greek reference works, use a five-case system. These scholars believe that, since the genitive and ablative were spelled identically, they should not be considered as separate.

Because this book is intended to be as user friendly as possible, we will consider both genitive and ablative under the broad heading "genitive." For those uses of the genitive called ablative by some scholars, the appropriate ablative designation is also given. The English translations of the genitives offered in this chapter are often paraphrases. They are meant to answer the question, What do you mean, of?

5.1. Genitives Describing a Noun

When genitives modify nouns, they may function in several relationships to that noun. Description is the basic idea of the genitive, and some (but not all) of these are descriptive.

5.1.1. Possessive Genitive or Relational Genitive

The **possessive genitive** is easy because of the English parallel. It identifies an owner.

Παῦλος καὶ Τιμόθεος δοῦλοι **Χριστοῦ Ἰησοῦ**.

Paul and Timothy, slaves **owned by Christ Jesus** (Phil. 1:1).

The **relational genitive** indicates a personal connection of something less than ownership between two persons. Usually kinship or friendship is involved. Sometimes Greek takes a shortcut and leaves out kinship terms, as in the third example, which omits γυνή.

Παῦλος ἀπόστολος **Χριστοῦ Ἰησοῦ**.

Paul an apostle **in relation to Christ Jesus** (Col. 1:1).

ἡ μήτηρ **αὐτοῦ** διετήρει πάντα τὰ ῥήματα.

The mother **related to him** treasured all these things (Luke 2:51).

Μαρία ἡ **τοῦ Κλωπᾶ**.

Mary, **Clopas's wife** (John 19:25).

5.1.2. Source Genitive or Subjective Genitive

The **source genitive** or the **ablative of source** indicates the origin or derivation of something or someone. In English, the word *from* often works. In the example that follows, the world could be thought of as possessing wisdom; however, source seems more likely. Sometimes you will not be able to decide clearly between options.

οὐχὶ ἐμώρανεν ὁ θεὸς τὴν σοφίαν **τοῦ κόσμου**;

Has God not made foolish the wisdom
coming from the world? (1 Cor. 1:20).

Quite closely related to the source genitive is the **subjective genitive**. When an **action noun** is modified by a genitive indicating the origin or instigator of the action, this is called a subjective genitive. An action noun implies some activity. *Baptism, hatred,* and *proclamation* are action nouns; *water, mother,* and *Scripture* are not. The title "subjective" is used because, if you recast the action noun as an action verb, the genitive modifier becomes the subject doing the action. (For example, *baptism* becomes *baptizes; hatred* becomes *hates; proclamation* becomes *proclaims*.) In the examples following, the second English example (in parentheses) shows how the Greek genitive serves as the subject for the action named.

τήν ἐπαγγελίαν **τοῦ πατρός**.

The promise **made by the Father** (Acts 1:4).

(The **Father** promised something.)

τὸ βάπτισμα **Ἰωάννου** ἐξ οὐρανοῦ ἦν;

Was the baptism **given by John** from heaven? (Luke 20:4).

(**John** baptized people. Was this from heaven?)

5.1.3. Objective Genitive

The logical opposite of the subjective genitive is the objective genitive. These two must be carefully distinguished. Think about the English sentence, "Jan has the love of God in her heart." Does this mean that Jan loves God or that Jan senses God's love toward her? Without a context, the meaning could go either way. In the Greek Testament these are usually easy to decipher, but not always.

When an action noun is modified by a genitive indicating the receiver or object of the action, this is called an **objective genitive**. The title "objective" is used because, if you recast the action noun into an action verb, the genitive modifier becomes the direct object receiving the action. In the following examples, the second English example (in parentheses) shows how the Greek genitive serves as the object of the action named.

τὸ μαρτύριον **τοῦ Χριστοῦ** ἐβεβαιώθη ἐν ὑμῖν.

Our testimony **about Christ** was confirmed to you (1 Cor. 1:6).

(We testified about **Christ**. It was confirmed to you.)

ἐν πίστει ζῶ τῇ **τοῦ υἱοῦ τοῦ θεοῦ.**

I live by faith **in the Son of God** (Gal. 2:20).

(I live by believing **the Son of God**.)

If you want a real challenge in this regard, think about Paul's phrase in 2 Corinthians 13:14: ἡ κοινωνία τοῦ ἁγίου πνεύματος. Did he mean, "fellowship produced by the Holy Spirit" (subjective genitive) or "fellowship with the Holy Spirit" (objective genitive)? Look at the context for clues.

5.1.4. Appositive Genitive or Content Genitive

You probably remember that an English appositive renames a noun: "My physician, Dr. Brown, is quite skillful." Sometimes an *of* phrase is used: "The city of Chicago is windy." In Greek, appositives usually belong to the same case as the noun they rename. Sometimes, however, an appositive is put in a genitive form. (The technical name for this is the **epexegetic genitive**. Others call it the **genitive of identity**.) For these the translational notion *that is* clarifies the relationship.

τὸν ἀρραβῶνα **τοῦ πνεύματος.**

The pledge, **that is, the Spirit** (2 Cor. 5:5).

τὰ κατώτερα μέρη **τῆς γῆς.**

The lower regions, **that is, the earth** (Eph. 4:9).

Closely related to apposition is the idea of contents, that which fills something. In English we may speak of a "can of corn" or a "videotape of cartoons." Greek did something similar with the **content genitive**, in which a noun being modified was a container of some kind.

σύροντες τὸ δίκτυον **τῶν ἰχθύων.**

Towing the net **[full] of fishes** (John 21:8).

5.1.5. Partitive Genitive

The genitive can rename something (see 5.1.4.), or a genitive noun can be the entire portion from which part has been taken or specified in some way. If I tell you that "half of the money was stolen," you understand that "money" is the entire portion; "half" is the specified part. Some Greek scholars call this the **ablative of the whole**. You can remember the **partitive genitive** easily by noting that some fraction (definite or indefinite) is involved.

πολλοὶ **τῶν ἀνθρώπων** ἀπέθανον ἐκ τῶν ὑδάτων.

Many **of the people** died from the waters (Rev. 8:11).

τοὺς πτωχοὺς **τῶν ἁγίων** τῶν ἐν Ἰερουσαλήμ.

The poor **who are part of the saints** in Jerusalem (Rom. 15:26).

5.1.6. Separation Genitive or Comparative Genitive

A physical or logical removal of one thing from another may be indicated by the **separation genitive** or **ablative of separation**. These are most commonly indicated by using the preposition ἀπό or ἐκ, as in the second example. Note the English *from* used in translation.

ξένοι **τῶν διαθηκῶν**.

Strangers **from the covenants** (Eph. 2:12).

οὓς δὲ σώζετε **ἐκ πυρὸς** ἁρπάζοντες.

But save others, snatching them **from the fire** (Jude 23).

When two or more objects are compared, they are distinguished or separated by some criterion. Greek uses the **comparative genitive**, or **ablative of comparison** for this. English uses something entirely different. You must use the English word *than* when translating this.

πολλῶν στρουθίων διαφέρετε ὑμεῖς.

You are more valuable **than many sparrows** (Matt. 10:31).

5.1.7. Adjective Genitive

In English we may refer equally to a "song of joy" or to a "joyful song." We can speak of a "house of logs" or a "log house." In both English or Greek, many attributes of nouns may be given equally in an adjective form or in genitive case form. Some grammarians refer to this as the **descriptive genitive** or the **attributive genitive**. If none of the previous categories (5.1.1.–6.) fits a particular genitive that modifies a noun you are studying, you can call it an **ad-**

jective genitive. In the examples that follow, the adjective genitive is rendered as an ordinary English adjective.

ἑαυτοῖς ποιήσατε φίλους ἐκ τοῦ μαμωνᾶ **τῆς ἀδικίας**.

Make friends for yourselves with **unrighteous** money (Luke 16:9).

ἵνα καταργηθῇ τὸ σῶμα **τῆς ἁμαρτίας**.

So that the **sinful** body might abolished (Rom. 6:6).

5.2. Genitives Describing a Verb

When genitives modify verbs, they are functioning in an adverbial relationship to the verb in some way.

5.2.1. Time or Place Genitive

The genitive, dative (or locative), and accusative cases can answer questions of time and place. Although classical Greek drew fine distinctions, it is best to think of all these cases in biblical Greek—genitive, dative (or locative), and accusative—as simply answering the question of when or where.

παράλαβε τὸ παιδίον καὶ τὴν μητέρα αὐτοῦ **νυκτὸς** καὶ ἀνεχώρησεν.

He took the child and his mother **in the night** and left (Matt. 2:14).

ἵνα βάψῃ τὸ ἄκρον τοῦ δακτύλου αὐτοῦ **ὕδατος**.

So that he can dip his fingertip **in water** (Luke 16:24).

5.2.2. Agent Genitive

Logically related to the notion of the subjective genitive and the source genitive (5.1.2), but functioning as an adverb, is the **agent genitive**, or **ablative of agency**. This is found only with **passive verbs**. The person responsible for the action is put in the genitive case, with the preposition διά or ὑπό preceeding. The English *by* is used in translation.

τὸ ἔλαττον **ὑπὸ τοῦ κρείττονος** εὐλογεῖται.

The lesser one is blessed **by the greater one** (Heb. 7:7).

(**The greater one** blesses the lesser one.)

5.2.3. Genitive of Direct Object

You learned long ago that the accusative is the proper case for the direct object. Some verbs, however, require a genitive direct object rather than an accusative one. Some Greek verbs take either a genitive or an accusative object. A dictionary can identify these verbs. Several kinds of relationships include verbs of this sort. In the first six categories that follow, notice that the verbs are all actions that persons (as opposed to things) are doing.

5.2.3.1. Verbs of perceiving or sensing. Ἀκούω (I hear) and γεύομαι (I taste) are examples.

ἐάν τι αἰτώμεθα κατὰ τὸ θέλημα αὐτοῦ ἀκούει **ἡμῶν**.

If we ask anything according to his will he hears **us** (1 John 5:14).

5.2.3.2. Verbs of touching or taking hold of. Ἅπτομαι (I take hold) and ἐπιλαμβάνομαι (I seize) are examples.

καὶ ἐπιλαβόμενος **τῆς χειρὸς** τοῦ τυφλοῦ.

And he seized **the hand** of the blind man (Mark 8:23).

5.2.3.3. Verbs of sharing in or eating. Μετέχω (I partake of) and μεταλαμβάνω (I share in) are examples.

οὐ δύνασθε **τραπέζης** κυρίου μετέχειν καὶ **τραπέζης** δαιμονίων.

You cannot partake of both the Lord's **table**
and the demons' **table** (1 Cor. 10:21).

5.2.3.4. Verbs of taking charge or ruling. Ἄρχω (I rule) and κυριεύω (I am master of) are examples.

οἱ βασιλεῖς τῶν ἐθνῶν κυριεύουσιν **αὐτῶν**.

The kings of the gentiles are masters over **them** (Luke 22:25).

5.2.3.5. Verbs of remembering. Μνημονεύω (I remember) and μιμνήσκομαι (I keep in mind) are examples.

μιμνήσκεσθε **τῶν δεσμίων** ὡς συνδεδεμένοι.

Keep in mind **the prisoners** as [their] fellow prisoners
(Heb. 13:3).

5.2.3.6. Verbs of desiring or despising. Ἐπιθυμέω (I desire) and καταφρονέω (I despise) are examples.

εἴ τις **ἐπισκοπῆς** ὀρέγεται, **καλοῦ ἔργου** ἐπιθυμεῖ.

If one longs to be **an overseer**, he desires **a good work** (1 Tim. 3:1).

5.2.3.7. Verbs of departing, removing, ceasing abstaining, missing, or lacking. Ἀφίστημι (I leave) and λείπω (I lack) are examples. This category implies separation. Notice that you can add the English word *from* to the ideas listed in heading 5.2.3.7.: depart from, remove from, and so forth. Those who use the ablative case category will think of these direct objects as being in the ablative case (rather than the genitive). Often such verbs are followed by a prepositional phrase beginning with ἀπό, ἐκ, or παρά, instead of a direct object.

εἰ δέ τις ὑμῶν λείπεται **σοφίας**, αἰτείτω **παρὰ** . . . **θεοῦ**.

But if someone lacks **wisdom**, let him ask from . . . God (Jas. 1:5).

5.2.4. Genitive Absolute

An absolute clause is logically connected to the rest of the sentence but syntactically disconnected. The most common genitive absolute in Greek consists of a noun or pronoun in the genitive case with a **participle** in concord (agreeing in gender, case, and number with that noun or pronoun). The genitive noun or pronoun functions as the subject of the action in the participle. The object of the action in the participle, if specified, takes the normal (accusative) case. Every genitive absolute functions in some circumstantial (adverbial) relationship to the main verb of the sentence (see 4.6.3.1.–8.). Typically genitive absolutes come first in a sentence.

ἔτι ἁμαρτωλῶν **ὄντων ἡμῶν** Χριστὸς ὑπὲρ ἡμῶν ἀπέθανεν.

While **we were** still sinners, Christ died for us (Rom. 5:8).

ἀναχωρησάντων δὲ **αὐτῶν** ἰδοὺ ἄγγελος κυρίου
φαίνεται κατ᾽ ὄναρ τῷ Ἰωσήφ.

But after **they departed**, behold, the Lord's angel
appeared to Joseph in a dream (Matt. 2:13).

In the Romans 5:8 example, the participle is a "be" verb. The participle subject (we), as required for a genitive absolute, is in the genitive case. "Be" verbs do not take direct objects but **subject complements** (in this case, "sinners") in the same case as the subject (see 1.2.2.5.). This is an unusual instance of a subject complement in the genitive case rather than the expected nominative.

In the second example, notice that the subject of the participle (they = the Magi) does not appear in the main body of the sentence. In fact, this could easily be rewritten as two separate sentences: "They departed. Then the Lord's angel appeared . . ." Ordinary participles (see section 4.6) are directly related to some word in the sentence, as in the following example. (Those warned and those returning are the same.)

χρηματισθέντες κατ᾽ ὄναρ . . . δι᾽ ἄλλης ὁδοῦ
ἀνεχώρησαν εἰς τὴν χώραν αὐτῶν.

Having been warned in a dream . . . they departed
to their own country another way (Matt. 2:12).

5.3. Genitives Describing an Adjective

In Greek, as in English, such adjectives as *full, worthy,* and *guilty* are often followed by an *of*-type phrase: full of joy, worthy of praise, guilty of murder. Such phrases limit the sense of the adjective by telling what the fulness or worthiness or guiltiness refers to. This category may be called **genitive of reference**. Greek adjectives that may be followed by such a genitive include μέστος, πλήρης, ἔνοχος, and ἄξιος.

εἵλκυσεν τὸ δίκτυον εἰς τὴν γῆν μεστὸν **ἰχθύων μεγάλων**.

He dragged to the land the net full **of large fish** (John 21:11).

In rare instances, the adjective modified by a genitive of reference is implied in a verb rather than in a separate adjective.

εἰς τὸ καταξιωθῆναι ὑμᾶς **τῆς βασιλείας** τοῦ θεοῦ.

For you to be counted worthy **of the kingdom** of God
(2 Thess. 1:5).

5.4. Genitives Following a Preposition

A number of prepositions are followed by a genitive (or ablative) object. As you may remember, some Greek prepositions take their object with more than one case form following. Those formal prepositions (see 2.2.3.1.) occurring exclusively with genitive (or ablative) objects are ἀντί, ἀπό, ἐκ, and πρό. Those occurring with either a genitive (or ablative) or an accusative object are διά, κατά, μετά, περί, ὑπέρ, and ὑπό. Those prepositions that may occur with either a genitive (or ablative) object or a dative (locative or instrumental) case object or an accusative object are ἐπί and παρά.

ἡμεῖς ὀφείλομεν **ὑπὲρ τῶν ἀδελφῶν** τὰς ψυχὰς θεῖναι.

We ought to lay down our lives **for the brothers** (1 John 3:16).

All the **functional prepositions** listed in section 2.2.3.1. are followed by genitive objects when they function as prepositions. Most genitive prepositional phrases have adverbial force, that is, they describe the action of the verb in some way. Sometimes the precise relationship is difficult to determine.

δεῖξόν μοι τὴν πίστιν σου **χωρὶς τῶν ἔργων**.

Show me your faith **apart from works** (James 2:18).

For preaching purposes, it is usually enough for you to translate the preposition accurately. An excellent discussion on translating Greek prepositions (with the genitive or otherwise) is Murray J. Harris's essay at the end of volume three of *The New International Dictionary of New Testament Theology*.

Summary of the Genitive

1. DESCRIBING A NOUN

POSSESSIVE OR RELATIONAL	
possessive genitive	δοῦλοι Χριστοῦ
relational genitive	μήτηρ αὐτοῦ
SOURCE OR SUBJECTIVE	
source genitive (ablative of source)	σοφίαν τοῦ κόσμου
subjective genitive	τὸ βάπτισμα Ἰωάννου
OBJECTIVE	
objective genitive	μαρτύριον τοῦ Χριστοῦ
APPOSITIVE OR CONTENT	
appositive genitive (epexegetic/identity)	μέρη τῆς γῆς
content genitive	δίκτυον τῶν ἰχθύων
PARTITIVE	
partitive genitive (ablative of the whole)	πτωχοὺς τῶν ἁγίων
SEPARATION OR COMPARATIVE	
separation genitive (ablative of separation)	ξένοι τῶν διαθηκῶν
comparative genitive (ablative of comparison)	πολλῶν στρουθίων διαφέρετε ὑμεῖς
ADJECTIVE	
adjective genitive (descriptive, attributive)	μαμωνᾶ τῆς ἀδικίας

2. DESCRIBING A VERB

TIME OR PLACE	ἵνα βάψῃ τὸ ἄκρον τοῦ δακτύλου αὐτοῦ ὕδατος
AGENT (ablative of agent)	τὸ ἔλαττον ὑπὸ τοῦ κρείττονος εὐλογεῖται

DIRECT OBJECT	
verbs of perceiving or sensing	ἀκούει ἡμῶν
verbs of touching or taking hold of	ἐπιλαβόμενος τῆς χειρὸς
verbs of sharing in or eating	τραπέζης κυρίου μετέχειν
verbs of taking charge or ruling	κυριεύουσιν αὐτῶν
verbs of remembering	μιμνήσκεσθε τῶν δεσμίων
verbs of desiring or despising	καλοῦ ἔργου ἐπιθυμει
verbs of departing, removing, ceasing, abstaining, missing, or lacking (ablative)	λείπεται σοφίας
GENITIVE ABSOLUTE	ἀναχωρησάντων δὲ αὐτῶν ἰδοὺ ἄγγελος κυρίου φαίνεται

3. DESCRIBING AN ADJECTIVE

genitive of reference	μεστὸν ἰχθύων

4. FOLLOWING A PREPOSITION

object of a formal preposition	ὑπὲρ τῶν ἀδελφῶν
object of an informal preposition	χωρὶς τῶν ἔργων

For Further Reading

Blass, F., and A. Debrunner. *A Greek Grammar of the New Testament and Other Early Christian Literature.* Trans. and rev. Robert W. Funk, 89–100. University of Chicago Press, 1961.

Brooks, James A., and Carlton L. Winbery. *Syntax of New Testament Greek,* 7–29. Washington: University Press of America, 1979.

Dana, H. E., and Julius R. Mantey. *A Manual Grammar of the Greek New Testament*, 72–83. New York: Macmillan Co., 1927.

Harris, Murray J. "Appendix: Prepositions and Theology in the Greek New Testament." In vol. 3 of *The New International Dictionary of New Testament Theology*. Colin Brown, gen. ed., 1171–1215. Grand Rapids: Zondervan Publishing House, 1978.

MacDonald, William G. *Greek Enchiridion: A Concise Handbook of Grammar for Translation and Exegesis*, 79–84. Peabody, Mass.: Hendrickson Publishers, 1986.

Moule, C. F. D. *An Idiom Book of New Testament.* 2nd ed., 36–47. Cambridge University Press, 1959.

Robertson, A. T. *A Grammar of the Greek New Testament in the Light of Historical Research*, 491–520. Nashville: Broadman Press, 1934.

Now Let's Apply!

All genitive forms (articles included with what they modify) from Matthew 4:1–11 and Philippians 1:3–11 are reproduced below. Determine what the case significance is for each one. Then write "yes" or "no" according to whether you believe each particular form is worth mention in a sermon. The first two for each text have been completed to help get you started

Matthew 4

GENITIVE FORM	CASE SIGNIFICANCE	SERMON MENTION?
Verse 1:		
τοῦ πνεύματος	agent (object of preposition)	yes
τοῦ διαβόλου	agent (object of preposition)	yes
Verse 3:		
τοῦ θεοῦ	_____	_____
Verse 4:		
στόματος	_____	_____
θεοῦ	_____	_____

Verse 5:

τοῦ ἱεροῦ

_____   _____

Verse 6:

τοῦ θεοῦ

_____   _____

αὐτοῦ

_____   _____

σοῦ

_____   _____

χειρῶν

_____   _____

σου

_____   _____

Verse 7:

σου

_____   _____

Verse 8:

τοῦ κόσμου

_____   _____

αὐτῶν

_____   _____

Verse 10:

σου

_____   _____

After you have completed the chart on Matthew 4:1–11, look back over your work. Circle the five genitive forms that you think are most interesting from the point of view of case and that you would consider giving sermonic attention. Can you justify your choices?

Philippians 1

GENITIVE FORM	CASE SIGNIFICANCE	SERMON MENTION?
Verse 3:		
μου	relationship	no
ὑμῶν	objective	no

Verse 4:

μου

πάντων ὑμῶν   _____   _____

χαρᾶς   _____   _____

Verse 5:

ὑμῶν   _____   _____

τῆς πρώτης ἡμέρας   _____   _____

τοῦ νῦν   _____   _____

Verse 6:

ἡμέρας   _____   _____

Χριστοῦ Ἰησοῦ   _____   _____

Verse 7:

πάντων ὑμῶν   _____   _____

μου   _____   _____

τοῦ εὐαγγελίου   _____   _____

μου   _____   _____

τῆς χάριτος   _____   _____

Verse 8:

μου   _____   _____

Χριστοῦ Ἰησοῦ   _____   _____

Verse 9:

ὑμῶν   _____   _____

Verse 10:

Χριστοῦ   _____   _____

Verse 11:

δικαιοσύνης   _____   _____

Ἰησοῦ Χριστοῦ   _____   _____

θεοῦ   _____   _____

After you have completed the chart on Philippians 1:3–11, look back over your work. Circle the five genitive forms that you think are most interesting from the point of view of case and that you would consider giving sermonic attention. Can you justify your choices?

<table>
<tr><td>

6

</td><td>

Patterns
in the Text

</td></tr>
</table>

$\mathbf{W}$e have now covered the important individual "trees" of the Greek landscape. It is time to look at the "forest" as a whole. One way contemporary Bible scholars think about this distinction is to note the difference between microstructure—analysis of the sentence and smaller units within sentences—and macrostructure—analysis of patterns that consider relationships beyond the sentence level. This study of macrostructure is similar to what linguists call discourse analysis. (See *Linguistics and New Testament Interpretation,* edited by David Alan Black and Kathleen Barnwell; *Linguistics and Biblical Interpretation,* by Peter Cotterell and Max Turner, and *The Grammar of Discourse,* by Robert Longacre).

The theory and practice of formal **discourse analysis** by professional linguists is relatively new; however, it has been practiced informally by exegetes and preachers for years. Whenever you hear someone say, "The key word for Philippians is joy," or "This is the climax of John's argument," you know that someone has been paying attention to macrostructure.

6.1. Paragraph Patterns

In most colleges and seminaries, the focus of the second year of Greek study is interpreting the sentence, for it is the sentence that communicates a complete idea (**microstructure**). However, few sentences are logically independent. They are interrelated to the other sentences in their paragraph, and, in fact, to all the sentences in the work to which they belong (**macrostructure**). As we noted at the beginning of this book, if you are going to use Greek responsibly, you need to learn to think paragraphs (1.3.).

6.1.1. Patterns Among Paragraph Sentences

Go back and review section 1.3.2. Typically a paragraph has three kinds of sentences: introductory sentence, development sentence, and summary sentence. Not only does this kind of analysis work for studying a single paragraph, but also for studying several paragraphs. Paragraphs are related to one another just as sentences in one paragraph are related. Paragraphs are the building blocks from which the entire discourse is built. Learn to use the Discourse Segmentation Apparatus of the fourth edition of the UBS Greek text. It will inform you of where editors and translators have differed on paragraph breaks, sentence breaks, and other segments of discourse within the text.

Consider the second paragraph of Philippians (1:3–11), using the exercise you did for chapter 1 as a guide. The paragraph is composed of three sentences. (For simplicity in this discussion, we are not counting as Greek sentences those punctuated with a colon; only those with a period are counted; see 2.2.1.)

The first sentence, although very long, is clearly introductory. Note that it has no initial conjunction. The theme of the whole paragraph is stated in this: "I thank God." Notice that within the first sentence, Paul focuses on the cause of his thanksgiving. The second sentence begins with the coordinate conjunction γάρ. This is certainly a development sentence. Here Paul states briefly another cause of thanksgiving. The third sentence begins with καί. This is another development sentence giving the content of Paul's thanksgiving. There is no summary sentence.

Now consider the third paragraph of Philippians (1:12–14). The paragraph is composed of one sentence. The sentence has the initial conjunction δέ. This connects the entire paragraph to the preceding paragraph. The vocative ἀδελφοί is Paul's grammatical signal that he is moving to a new paragraph. The theme of the paragraph is the advance of the gospel (see the end of v. 12).

6.1.2. Structure Marker Patterns

Prepositions, relative pronouns, coordinate conjunctions, and subordinate conjunctions are the important structure markers within a paragraph. Go back and review section 2.2.3. In the exegesis process, you begin with a paragraph flow—that is, if you follow the guidelines given in this book. At the beginning of the process, you make preliminary decisions about the relationship between sentences and clauses. Later, you confirm your earlier decisions. Go back and review the example of James 1:2–8 that was the model for a paragraph flow in section 2.3.5. Notice how the structure markers (in capital letters) help reveal the development of James's thinking.

An important part of preparing to preach from a paragraph is to discover the sentence patterns within the paragraph. How can you know what is central to an author's thinking in his paragraph unless you have considered his introductory sentences, development sentences, and summary sentences?

6.2. Narrative Patterns

Bible students have often noted that God's revelation of Himself came to humanity through events as well as through words. The written record of those events is always told from a particular perspective. Bible books have been shaped and written to communicate what the human author thought was important. When you are studying a narrative for sermon preparation, you will usually choose an entire pericope instead of a single paragraph (see section 1.3.1.).

Because the first five books of the New Testament are mainly narrative, it is helpful to be aware of narrative patterns that are common to all such literature—whether fictional (such as the parables) or historical (such as the birth accounts). Since the 1970s, New Testament scholars have increasingly relied on the techniques of narrative criticism in coming to a better understanding of the message of biblical texts.

6.2.1. Questions to Ask a Narrative

The following outline suggests the kinds of questions you may use to help determine narrative patterns within a pericope. You may think of other questions that might help you see how narrative is developed. Don't be surprised if the following list reminds you of the kinds of questions your high school or college literature teacher asked you to use in studying a short story or novel or some other narrative form. By the way, most of this work can be done from your English Bible, without reference to the Greek.

- What is the setting?
- Who is the subject? (Who is the main character?)
- Is there an object? (Does someone or something receive the action?)
- Is there an opponent? (Is there an enemy to the subject?)
- How does the dialogue develop? (How many people talk? Are they friendly or hostile? Do the speakers seem to be understanding each other?)
- What about character development? (Does any character change in attitude or understanding?)
- Is there any conflict resolution?
- What is the emotional tone of the narrative?
- Is the narrator's presence felt?
- What contrasts are developed? (Every narrative has them!) Some of the most important ones are as follows:

good/evil	union/separation	gain/loss
help/hurt	love/hate	life/death

- Where is the climax (or peak) of the story?

6.2.2. Example: The Rich Young Ruler (Matt. 19:16–30)

- Setting: somewhere on the road to Jerusalem during Jesus' final days before the triumphal entry (see Matt. 19:1–2; 20:17).
- Subject: Jesus.
- Object: the rich young ruler.
- Opponent: none (the apostles are secondary figures).
- Dialogue is in two parts: (1) Jesus and the man—a strong question-and-answer format. Both ask questions. (2) Jesus and the disciples—they ask a question; Jesus answers briefly; they respond; Jesus gives a lengthy explanation.
- Character development: the young man grows in enlightenment and makes a calculated decision.
- Conflict resolution: the young man's decision resolves his personal situation. The apostles are left trying to work out what it means to leave everything for Christ's sake.
- Emotional tone: the sadness of the young man and the astonishment of the disciples are prominently mentioned.

- Narrator: his presence is minimal. (We aren't told some things that the narrator obviously knows, such as how the young man was recognized as wealthy.)
- Contrasts: gain/loss; material wealth/treasure in heaven; leaving things in this life/receiving eternal life; first/last.
- Climax: verse 22, the surprising decision of the young man. The entire pericope hinges on this action.

How does an awareness of these narrative features help you understand the text? We see that Matthew is concerned with showing Jesus during His final days of ministry engaged in vigorous dialogue, reaching out first to the young man, then to the Twelve. We also see that enlightenment does not mean that someone will decide to follow Jesus. The astonishment of the disciples at Jesus' teaching should be given proper notice: this was a surprising word (recorded by a former tax collector who had left all his wealth to follow Jesus).

The contrasts suggest some of the great overarching human concerns of all time. People of today certainly relate to the notion of gain/loss. You may be able to use these contrasts as a major feature of your sermon development. You may be able to plan your sermon climax so as to echo the narrative climax of the pericope.

6.3. Compositional Patterns

In his *New Testament Exposition*, Walter Liefeld not only discussed narrative pattern, but also twelve compositional patterns often found in didactic (nonnarrative) material (pp. 60–72). Narrative passages may certainly contain these as well. These patterns may often be determined without reference to the Greek text.

6.3.1. Comparison or Contrast

This pattern is frequent (see 2.4.3., 5.1.6.). The following are obvious examples: Christ and Adam, Romans 5:12–21; the works of the flesh and the fruit of the Spirit, Galatians 5:19–23; Jesus and Melchizedek, Hebrews 7:1–28; faith and works, James 2:14–26. In such a pattern, discover both how the items compared are alike and how they are different.

6.3.2. Repetition

This is a powerful pattern for noting emphasis (see 2.4.1.). Jesus loved to use this device, but it is found in other places. The eight *blessed*s of Matthew 5 followed by the repeated *you have heard that it was said*s are part of what makes the Sermon on the Mount so effective. Similarly, in Matthew 23:1–32 Jesus pronounced *woe to you* on the Pharisees seven times with great effect. Paul's overall outline of 1 Corinthians can be traced by his repetition of *now concerning* (macrostructure). Another example is the seven *ones* of Ephesians 4:4–6 (microstructure).

6.3.3. Continuity

Continuity is a matter of continuing a theme without repeating a word or phrase. For example, 1 Corinthians 12-14 is acknowledged as a single unit on the theme "spiritual gifts." In Colossians 3:18–4:1, the theme is obviously rules for relationships in a Christian household. Recognizing the continuity of a passage can become the basis for developing a series of sermons on the underlying theme.

6.3.4. Climax

When writers are developing arguments, they often write so that the conclusion or climax becomes the focal point. For example, Paul's argument on the universality of sin is brought to a climax in Romans 3:20; the climax to his discussion of his personal struggle with sin comes in Romans 7:24–25. And the great hymn to Christ in Philippians reaches a climax in 2:11.

6.3.5. Cruciality

Cruciality can be defined as a turning point in a narrative or argument. When a crucial statement is omitted, the force of the narrative or argument changes. A famous example in narrative is Luke 9:51, the statement that Jesus set out resolutely for Jerusalem. Luke means for his readers to note that from this point on, Jesus had the crucifixion uppermost in his mind, during everything he said and did. In Paul's discussion of spiritual gifts (1 Corinthians 12–14), the statement "now I will show you the most excellent way" (12:31b) is of crucial importance. Without it we are at a loss to understand the relationship between gifts and love.

6.3.6. Interchange

This pattern is one of going back and forth between one subject and another. Sometimes it is coupled with the device of comparison or contrast (see 6.3.1.). A good example is found in Romans 14:1–3, Paul's discussion of the weak and the strong. He begins with the weak (v. 1), moves to the strong (v. 2a), then back to the weak (v. 2b), then to the strong (v. 3a), and so on (microstructure). Luke 1–2 alternates between John and Jesus (macrostructure): first comes the announcement of John's birth; then the announcement about Jesus; next comes the account of John's birth; then the story of Jesus' birth. Luke uses this pattern to make the narrative more interesting. He wants the reader to compare these two unusual births carefully.

6.3.7. Particularization

This is a matter of moving from a general statement to specific examples or illustrations. Jesus' statement about not doing acts of righteousness before people is followed by three examples: giving, praying, and fasting (Matt. 6:1–18). According to some interpreters, Paul's general statement that "the fruit of the Spirit is love" is followed by examples of how love is expressed: joy, peace, patience . . . (Gal. 5:22–23). The statement that all Christians have different gifts is particularized in the verses that follow (Rom. 12:6–8). Great preachers learn the skill of particularization early in their careers. Recognizing particularization in a biblical text makes contemporary application much easier.

6.3.8. Generalization

This is the opposite of particularization. After citing several examples, a writer may give the principle that covers them all. The Book of Acts is famous for giving a number of such summary statements; one example is Acts 12:24. James 5:13–16a lists several situations that call for prayer, followed by the principle that a righteous Christian's prayer is powerful and effective.

6.3.9. Cause to Effect (Result)

In John 11 Lazarus was raised from the dead; the effect was that Jewish authorities plotted to kill Jesus. In Philippians 1:12–14 Paul listed the surprising effect of his imprisonment: the spread of the gospel. Cause to effect occurs everywhere in literature. In Greek, words such as ἵνα and ὥστε are often signals that the writer is telling the effect (result) of an action.

6.3.10. Substantiation

This is the opposite of cause to effect. Often a writer tells of an event and then states the reason or the grounds for the event. In Greek, ὅτι is often a signal that the writer is telling the cause of an action. An excellent example is Romans 8:28–30. Romans 8:28 is very well known. However, verse 29 begins with ὅτι. The basis of God's working all things for good is certainly His predestinating care for those He will ultimately glorify.

6.3.11. Progression

This pattern is found when an argument is moving forward step by step. The difference between this and continuity (see 6.3.3.) is that in the progression pattern, the argument advances; in the continuity pattern, facts related to the theme are stated without any real logical development. A good example of progression (tied to repetition) is found in Paul's argument in Romans 1 concerning the degenerating effects of human sin ("God gave them over" in Rom. 1:24,26,28).

6.3.12. Radiation

This last notion is a kind of "punt" category. When material seems to be organized loosely around a theme, but the development is in several directions, the pattern is called radiation. When none of the other categories fits, material can be put into this category. An example is 1 Corinthians 15, in which Paul discusses various aspects of the resurrection by making a series of comments that do not seem to relate logically to one another. Another instance is found in James 1, with the general theme of trials and temptations developed along several lines (see 2.4.). Commentators have despaired at determining the logic of 1 John.

Liefeld closed his discussion of compositional patterns with the following words: "It is already apparent that when we discipline ourselves to be alert for these twelve compositional patterns we accomplish two things. First, we are likely to find a pattern that itself can form the basis for a sermon outline. Second, and more important, we will tend to follow closely the author's own direction of thought, rather than to superimpose our own impressions" (p. 72).

6.4. Word Patterns

Within a particular paragraph or pericope of text, word patterns sometimes exist that merit close attention. The most important of these patterns follow.

6.4.1. Synonym Patterns

Often in a single paragraph, a writer selects his vocabulary using words of **overlapping relations** (see 6.5.5.) for the sake of variety rather than because of any subtle differences in meaning between the words. Many New Testament scholars believe that the alternation between forms of ἀγαπάω and φιλέω in John 21:15–17 is due to John's variation in usage rather than to any real difference in meaning between the verbs in this context.

6.4.2. Semantic Fields

Careful attention to the UBS *Lexicon* will alert you to words that are closely related to the same concept. The nouns ἀρνίον and πρόβατον belong to the same general semantic domain (animals) but are not synonymous (lamb and sheep). In John 21:15–17, however, the two are used in such a way that we know the **semantic domain** has changed to another field (classes of persons). They have precisely the same referent (follower of Christ) and are synonymous in the context (see 6.5.3. for further explanation).

6.4.3. Antonyms

Some writers like to use word pairs that are opposites. John is well known for this. The most commonly found antonyms in the New Testament are negatives and positives (see 2.4.2.). Word contrasts are another kind of antonym (see 6.2.1, 6.3.1.). Awareness of this can help one understand the way contrasts are developed. For example, in Romans 5:1-11 there are several such pairs: ungodly/righteous; sinners/good; death/life.

6.4.4. Cognates

These are words that share the same Greek stem but may have different meanings. They may be placed near each other for literary effect. Philippians 2:17-20 has two excellent examples: first, verbs sharing the stem χαιρ- (rejoice) occur four times in verses 17–18; second, the stem ψυχ- (soul) is repeated in verses 19–20.

6.4.5. Alliteration

Occasionally, authors of the Greek Testament used this device. Hebrews 1:1 contains an outstanding example: πολυμερῶς καὶ πολυπρόπως πάλαι ὁ θεὸς λαλήσας τοῖς πατράσιν ἐν τοῖς προφήταις. I recommend that you use alliteration only as often in your sermon points as the New Testament authors did in their writings.

6.4.6. Chiasm

A frequent word pattern is the chiasm, consisting of four elements. In this pattern, the first and fourth elements are similar; the second and third are also similar. Sometimes this is called the a-b-b'-a' structure. 1 Corinthians 7:3 is an example:

"The husband (a) must fulfill his marital duty to his wife (b),

and likewise the wife (b') to her husband (a').

The reason this is called chiasm is because the Greek letter chi (X) results if you draw lines connecting the two *a*'s and the two *b*'s on the two lines. Recent studies have found even more elaborate chiasms (for example, a-b-c-d-d'-c'-b'-a') in many texts, sometimes extending for several verses. While such chiasms may be interesting from the point of view of literary analysis, they probably have little value in sermon preparation.

6.5. Supplement: Introduction to Word Study

In 1961 James Barr published *The Semantics of Biblical Language*. In many ways this work revolutionized the way New Testament scholars think about understanding Greek words. Two recent works that are helpful in incorporating a linguistic approach to Greek are David Alan Black's *Linguistics for Students of New Testament Greek: A Survey of Basic Concepts and Applications* and Moisés Silva's *Biblical Words and Their Meaning: An Introduction to Lexical Semantics*. Each of these is worth reading. The following discussion presents several important concepts accepted in a modern linguistic approach to Greek word studies.

6.5.1. Etymology vs. *Usus Loquendi*

A hundred years ago, it was widely believed that the meaning of Greek words could best be determined by studying the historical development of the word through time and the meaning of the component parts (etymological or diachronic word study). Recent study has emphasized synchronic word study. This approach is more effective in determining a word's meaning. The synchronic approach considers the way or ways a word is used at a particular point in time by native speakers of a language. The synchronic approach alone fully acknowledges that individual speakers or writers select their own usage of a word (the *usus loquendi*) from the meanings current in their own time.

In the 1940s, "Tom is gay" meant "Tom is happy and carefree." Today the same sentence means something entirely different. While it is interesting to know the origins and history of the word *gay*, this has nothing to do with the way a current speaker uses the word. One cannot impose a contemporary meaning on a 1940s text—or vice versa.

The goal of word studies in the Greek New Testament must focus on *usus loquendi* (use in location), not on the etymology of the word. How does this writer use this word in this context? The original meaning of a word is not the real meaning unless that meaning corresponds with the way the word is currently used.

6.5.2. Clarity vs. Ambiguity

We take it as a given that the goal of writing or speech is usually to communicate with clarity. However, language is often ambiguous; that is, more than one sense is often possible for a word, phrase, or sentence. Does "I love flying planes" mean "I like watching planes as they fly through the air" or "I enjoy piloting a plane"? Does "I speak to you as a father" suggest that I have fatherly feelings toward you or that I respect you as if you were my father? This kind of ambiguity can be dealt with as a matter of exegesis. Usually such ambiguity is unintended, since it is a matter of note that language is often used carelessly. Of course, some statements in the New Testament that we think are ambiguous may seem so due to our lack of familiarity with Greek usage rather than to careless use by the original author.

A word itself can be ambiguous. *Stock* in English can refer to cattle on a ranch or to the contents of a grocery store. Thus, "Jane has a lot of stock" is ambiguous without a larger context. (Maybe Jane's stock is on Wall Street.) This kind of ambiguity is due to what is called polysemy. This simply means that a single word may refer to more than one area of meaning. Many jokes and puns are based on such ambiguity.

"Jane hit a run" and "Jane's stockings have a run" show that often very little context can clarify a polysemous word. In a specific context, only one sense for a word is meant by an author. Little evidence of deliberate word ambiguity in the New Testament exists. Context serves to eliminate multiple meanings. Word studies should clarify the sense of a polysemous word. For example, πρεσβύτερος (elder) may refer either to a religious official in a church or synagogue or to an age category, but not to both at once. This observation is true even if a minimum age was required for admission to the religious office.

6.5.3. Word vs. Concept

Every language has several words used to discuss a given concept. For example, the concept "attractive young woman" might include the following currently used English adjectives: *gorgeous, pretty, knockout, beautiful.* The same is true with Greek. The notion "right with God" includes at least the following: δίκαιος, ἀγαθός, καλός, and καθαρός. We cannot understand what the New Testament writers mean by "right with God" by studying δίκαιος alone. Two tools helpful for discovering words related in concept are Colin Brown's *New International Dictionary of New Testament Theology* and the United Bible Societies' *The Greek-English Lexicon of the New Testament Based on Semantic Domains.*

Beware of treating an individual Greek word as if it alone represents a concept. No word can be fully understood without giving attention to other terms in the same **semantic field**.

6.5.4. Symbol vs. Sense vs. Referent

What is a word? Go back and review section 1.1. of this book. There we observed that at one level a word is a spoken or written symbol. As you read this and encounter the English printed word *dragon,* it is symbolized by six Roman letters: d-r-a-g-o-n. Why not spell it d-h-r-a-g-g-i-n or δ-ρ-α-γ-ω-ν? This is merely an arbitrary symbol and is incidental to the meaning. We also noted syntactical words, that is, the variant spellings a lexical entry (dictionary word) may have in a sentence. In English sentences, *dragon* has four possible spellings: *dragon, dragon's, dragons,* and *dragons'.* Word studies do not usually focus on these matters, although the Bauer-Arndt-Gingrich-Danker *Lexicon* gives information about many of them. Only an analytical lexicon or analytical concordance registers all the syntactical words in the Greek Testament.

Beyond the level of symbol and syntactical variants is the **sense** or mental content that comes to mind when you read or hear the symbol *dragon* (or *dragon's, dragons,* or *dragons'*). An image comes into your head (large scaly fire-breathing beast that flies). The difference between symbol and sense is the difference between form and content. Obviously, in dealing with word study we are much more concerned with the sense than the symbol. Understanding possible senses (meanings) of a word is basic to word study.

However, there is often another level, that of **referent** or the extralinguistic thing denoted—that which is in the world and outside the realm of language. Referents are determined by the speaker or writer. For example, in Revelation, *dragon* refers to Satan. A good example of how this principle is important in word studies is the Greek word παράκλητος. The sense of the word is "helper." In 1 John 2:1, it refers to Jesus as a helper; elsewhere in the New Testament it refers to the Holy Spirit as a helper. Our understanding of παράκλητος is seriously flawed if we do not take its referent into account in such texts.

Another New Testament example is σῷζω. This verb means to release someone from dangerous circumstances and to restore to safety. In Matthew 8:25, the verb refers to release from dangerous physical circumstances. In Matthew 1:21, the same verb refers to release from the power and guilt of sin. Obviously, word study focuses even more on the reference of the word than on the sense. From a practical point of view, however, often sense and reference may be thought of together under the general heading "meaning."

6.5.5. Synonyms

Absolute synonyms do not exist in language. There are, however, words that overlap in meaning in some contexts. Take *high* and *tall.* Consider two sentences: "That mountain is high" and "That mountain is tall." The two words are synonymous in this context. But also consider the sentences "John is high" and "John is tall." The two words now have very different senses. To talk about such words, the terminology **overlapping relations** is helpful. Thus, in English, *high* and *tall* have overlapping relations; that is, they are synonymous in certain contexts, though not in others. Two Greek examples: ἀγαπάω—φιλέω (I love); πνεῦμα—ψυχή (self).

Other words are related in a way best described as **contiguous relations** or improper synonymy. In English *hop* and *skip* may refer to forward movement using the legs. But to say that Jan is hopping is not the same as saying the she is skipping; the two are not used interchangeably in everyday speech. Still, the two words share some semantic features; they are in the same semantic field. Two Greek examples: ἱμάτιον (coat)—χιτών (shirt); ὄχλος (crowd)—ἐκκλησία (church).

Another relationship between words with similar senses is that of **inclusive relations** or hyponymy, in which one word includes another. Our word *food* includes both steak and cherry pie. The more general word is called the superordinate; the more specific word is the hyponym. Two Greek examples: αἰτέω (I ask)—δέομαι (I pray); ἄνθρωπος (human)—υἱός (son).

To summarize, it helps greatly in doing a word study to discover other words with which the word may have an overlapping, contiguous, or hyponymous relationship. The UBS *Lexicon* is the best resource for this.

6.5.6. Denotation vs. Connotation

The denotation of a word is the meaning (or meanings) a word has for all native speakers of a language. The associations normally conjured up by a spoken or written word are its denotations. (If only a single sense comes to most people's minds when the word is without a context this is called the unmarked meaning.) However, many words acquire a special meaning for a limited group of speakers. Often this special meaning is one of emotional content. These are its connotations. For example, in English *child* and *babe* are nouns of overlapping relations; they are synonymous in some contexts. *Child* has a rather negative value if a young woman tells her friend, "Joe is such a child," when speaking about a recent date. *Babe* has a different emotional value if Joe tells his friend about the same experience, "What a babe!" In John 21:5 παιδία (children) apparently has a negative connotation, whereas in John 1:12, τέκνα (children) is positive. In doing word studies, one must be alert to the possibility that a particular word may be used with a special connotation.

6.5.7. Idioms

Many phrases mean something other than the sum of their parts. "Hit the sack," "touch and go," and "under the weather" are examples. In your word studies be alert to the possibility of idioms. An easy example is σὰρξ καὶ αἷμα (flesh and blood = natural human life). The UBS *Lexicon* is especially valuable for identifying and translating idioms.

For Further Reading

Barr, James. *The Semantics of Biblical Language*. Oxford: Oxford University Press, 1961.

Bauer, Walter. *A Greek-English Lexicon of the New Testament and Other Eraly Christian Literature*. Trans. and adapted by William F. Arndt and F. Wilbur Gingrich. 2d ed. Rev. and augmented by F. Wilbur Gingrich and Frederick W. Danker. Chicago: University of Chicago Press, 1979.

Black, David Alan. *Linguistics for Students of New Testament Greek: A Survey of Basic Concepts and Applications*. Grand Rapids: Baker Book House, 1988.

Black, David Alan, and Kathleen Barnwell, eds. *Linguistics and New Testament Interpretation*. Nashville: Broadman Press, 1992.

Bock, Darrell L. "New Testament Word Analysis." In *Introducing New Testament Interpretations,* ed. Scot McKnight, 97–113. Grand Rapids: Baker Book House, 1989.

Brown, Colin, ed. *New International Dictionary of New Testament Theology.* 4 vols. Grand Rapids: Zondervan Publishing House, 1975–86.

Carson, Donald A. *Exegetical Fallacies,* 25–66. Grand Rapids: Baker Book House, 1984.

Cotterell, Peter, and Max Turner. *Linguistics and Biblical Interpretation.* Downers Grove, Ill.: InterVarsity Press, 1989.

Liefeld, Walter L. *New Testament Exposition: From Text to Sermon.* Grand Rapids: Zondervan Publishing House, 1984.

Longacre, Robert E. *The Grammar of Discourse.* New York: Plenum Press, 1983.

Louw, Johannes P. *Semantics of New Testament Greek.* Philadelphia: Fortress Press, 1982.

Louw, Johannes P., and Eugene A. Nida, eds. *Greek-English Lexicon of the New Testament Based on Semantic Domains.* New York: United Bible Societies, 1988.

Silva, Moisés. *Biblical Words and Their Meaning: An Introduction to Lexical Semantics.* Grand Rapids: Zondervan Publishing House, 1983.

Now Let's Apply!

Turn to the paragraph flow for Matthew 4:1–11 and Philippians 1:3–11 that you did as part of the homework for chapter 2. (Go back and do this now if you have not done so.)

1. Verify the decisions you made about the three kinds of sentences within these paragraphs: introductory, development, summary (2.2.1.).

2. Review the structure markers that introduce clauses. Notice whether any repetition or other patterns are apparent (2.2.3.).

3. Review the decisions you made about clause functions (2.3.4.). Make any corrections needed to your paragraph flow.

Matthew 4:1–11 is an outstanding narrative text. Take a fresh look at the temptation by answering some narrative questions about it.

1. Setting:

2. Subject:

3. Object:

4. Opponent:

5. Dialogue:

6. Character development:

7. Conflict resolution:

8. Emotional tone:

9. Narrator's presence: (Hint: What does the narrator know that ordinarily would be difficult to know? Where do you suppose he got his knowledge?)

10. Contrasts:

11. Climax:

12. Summary: In what ways does a focus on narrative pattern help you understand this paragraph?

Go back through your paragraph flow of Paul's prayer in Philippians 1:3–11. On the lines below, note verse references for any of the twelve patterns discussed in this chapter that you can find.

Comparison or contrast:

Repetition:

Continuity:

Climax:

Cruciality:

Interchange:

Particularization:

Generalization:

Cause to Effect (Result):

Substantiation:

Progression:

Radiation:

Investigate Matthew 4:1–11 and Philippians 1:3–11 from the perspective of word patterns. List the results of your investigation below.

Matthew 4:1–11

Synonym Patterns:

Antonyms:

Cognates:

Alliteration:

Chiasm:

Summary of your study of word patterns:

Philippians 1:3–11

Synonym Patterns:

Semantic Fields:

Antonyms:

Cognates:

Alliteration:

Chiasm:

Summary of your study of word patterns:

Answer Key

Chapter 1

Matthew 4

¹τότε ὁ Ἰησοῦς (subject) <u>ἀνήχθη</u> (P) εἰς τὴν ἔρημον ὑπὸ τοῦ πνεύματος, <u>πειρασθῆναι</u> (P) ὑπὸ τοῦ διαβόλου. CPLX

²καὶ <u>νηστεύσας</u> (T) ἡμέρας (direct object) τεσσεράκοντα καὶ νύκτας τεσσεράκοντα ὕστερον <u>ἐπείνασεν</u> (I). CPLX

³καὶ <u>προσελθὼν</u> ὁ <u>πειράζων</u> (subject) <u>εἶπεν</u> αὐτῷ (indirect object), εἰ υἱὸς <u>εἶ</u> (B) τοῦ θεοῦ, <u>εἰπὲ</u> ἵνα οἱ λίθοι (subject) οὗτοι ἄρτοι (subject complement) <u>γένωνται</u> (B). CPLX

⁴ὁ δὲ <u>ἀποκριθεὶς εἶπεν</u>, <u>γέγραπται</u> (P), οὐκ ἐπ' ἄρτῳ μόνῳ <u>ζήσεται</u> (I) ὁ ἄνθρωπος (subject), ἀλλ' ἐπὶ παντὶ ῥήματι <u>ἐκπορευομένῳ</u> (I) διὰ στόματος θεοῦ. CPLX

⁵τότε <u>παραλαμβάνει</u> (T) αὐτὸν ὁ διάβολος (subject) εἰς τὴν ἁγίαν πόλιν, καὶ <u>ἔστησεν</u> (T) αὐτὸν (direct object) ἐπὶ τὸ πτερύγιον τοῦ ἱεροῦ, ⁶καὶ <u>λέγει</u> αὐτῷ, εἰ υἱὸς <u>εἶ</u> (B) τοῦ θεοῦ, <u>βάλε</u> (T) σεαυτὸν (direct object) κάτω· <u>γέγραπται</u> γὰρ ὅτι τοῖς ἀγγέλοις (direct object) αὐτοῦ <u>ἐντελεῖται</u> περὶ σοῦ καὶ ἐπὶ χειρῶν <u>ἀροῦσίν</u> (T) σε, μήποτε <u>προσκόψῃς</u> (T) πρὸς λίθον τὸν πόδα σου. C-C

⁷<u>ἔφη</u> αὐτῷ ὁ Ἰησοῦς, πάλιν <u>γέγραπται</u>, οὐκ <u>ἐκπειράσεις</u> (T) κύριον (direct object) τὸν θεόν σου. CPLX

⁸πάλιν <u>παραλαμβάνει</u> (T) αὐτὸν (direct object) ὁ διάβολος (subject) εἰς ὄρος ὑψηλὸν λίαν, καὶ <u>δείκνυσιν</u> (T) αὐτῷ (indirect object) πάσας τὰς βασιλείας (direct object) τοῦ κόσμου καὶ τὴν

δόξαν αὐτῶν, ⁹καὶ <u>εἶπεν</u> αὐτῷ, ταῦτά σοι πάντα <u>δώσω</u> ἐὰν <u>πεσὼν</u> <u>προσκυνήσῃς</u> μοι. C-C

¹⁰τότε <u>λέγει</u> αὐτῷ ὁ Ἰησοῦς, <u>ὕπαγε</u>, Σατανᾶ· <u>γέγραπται</u> γάρ, κύριον (direct object) τὸν θεόν σου <u>προσκυνήσεις</u> καὶ αὐτῷ (direct object) μόνῳ <u>λατρεύσεις</u> (T). C-C

¹¹τότε <u>ἀφίησιν</u> (T) αὐτὸν ὁ διάβολος, καὶ ἰδοὺ ἄγγελοι <u>προσῆλθον</u> (I) καὶ <u>διηκόνουν</u> (I) αὐτῷ (direct object). CPND

Philippians 1

³<u>εὐχαριστῶ</u> (P) τῷ θεῷ (direct object) μου ἐπὶ πάσῃ τῇ μνείᾳ ὑμῶν, ⁴πάντοτε ἐν πάσῃ δεήσει μου ὑπὲρ πάντων ὑμῶν μετὰ χαρᾶς τὴν δέησιν (direct object) <u>ποιούμενος</u> (T), ⁵ἐπὶ τῇ κοινωνίᾳ ὑμῶν εἰς τὸ εὐαγγέλιον ἀπὸ τῆς πρώτης ἡμέρας ἄχρι τοῦ νῦν, ⁶<u>πεποιθὼς</u> (T) αὐτὸ τοῦτο (direct object), ὅτι ὁ <u>ἐναρξάμενος</u> (subject, T) ἐν ὑμῖν ἔργον ἀγαθὸν <u>ἐπιτελέσει</u> ἄχρι ἡμέρας Χριστοῦ Ἰησοῦ· ⁷καθὼς <u>ἐστιν</u> (B) δίκαιον ἐμοὶ τοῦτο <u>φρονεῖν</u> (T) ὑπὲρ πάντων ὑμῶν, διὰ τὸ <u>ἔχειν</u> με ἐν τῇ καρδίᾳ ὑμᾶς, ἔν τε τοῖς δεσμοῖς μου καὶ ἐν τῇ ἀπολογίᾳ καὶ βεβαιώσει τοῦ εὐαγγελίου συγκοινωνούς μου τῆς χάριτος πάντας ὑμᾶς <u>ὄντας</u> (B). CPLX

⁸μάρτυς (subject complement) γάρ μου ὁ θεός (subject), ὡς <u>ἐπιποθῶ</u> (T) πάντας ὑμᾶς ἐν σπλάγχνοις Χριστοῦ Ἰησοῦ. CPLX

⁹καὶ τοῦτο <u>προσεύχομαι</u>, ἵνα ἡ ἀγάπη (subject) ὑμῶν ἔτι μᾶλλον καὶ μᾶλλον <u>περισσεύῃ</u> ἐν ἐπιγνώσει καὶ πάσῃ αἰσθήσει, ¹⁰εἰς τὸ <u>δοκιμάζειν</u> ὑμᾶς τὰ <u>διαφέροντα</u>, ἵνα <u>ἦτε</u> (B) εἰλικρινεῖς (subject complement) καὶ ἀπρόσκοποι εἰς ἡμέραν Χριστοῦ, ¹¹<u>πεπληρωμένοι</u> (P) καρπὸν (direct object = "retained object") δικαιοσύνης τὸν διὰ Ἰησοῦ Χριστοῦ εἰς δόξαν καὶ ἔπαινον θεοῦ. CPLX

Chapter 2

Matthew 4:1–11

¹τότε ὁ Ἰησοῦς <u>ἀνήχθη</u> | εἰς τὴν ἔρημον | ὑπὸ τοῦ πνεύματος, πειρασθῆναι | ὑπὸ τοῦ διαβόλου (I). ²καὶ <u>νηστεύσας</u> ἡμέρας τεσσεράκοντα καὶ νύκτας τεσσεράκοντα ὕστερον <u>ἐπείνασεν</u> (D). ³| καὶ <u>προσελθὼν</u> ὁ <u>πειράζων</u> <u>εἶπεν</u> αὐτῷ, | εἰ υἱὸς εἶ τοῦ θεοῦ, <u>εἰπὲ</u> ἵνα οἱ λίθοι οὗτοι ἄρτοι <u>γένωνται</u> (D). ⁴ὁ | δὲ <u>ἀποκριθεὶς</u> <u>εἶπεν</u>, <u>γέγραπται</u>, οὐκ | ἐπ' ἄρτῳ μόνῳ <u>ζήσεται</u> ὁ ἄνθρωπος, | ἀλλ' | ἐπὶ παντὶ ῥήματι <u>ἐκπορευομένῳ</u> | διὰ στόματος θεοῦ (D). ⁵τότε <u>παραλαμβάνει</u> αὐτὸν ὁ διάβολος | εἰς τὴν ἁγίαν πόλιν, | καὶ <u>ἔστησεν</u> αὐτὸν | ἐπὶ τὸ

πτερύγιον τοῦ ἱεροῦ, ⁶ | καὶ <u>λέγει</u> αὐτῷ, | εἰ υἱὸς <u>εἶ</u> τοῦ θεοῦ, <u>βάλε</u> σεαυτὸν κάτω· <u>γέγραπται</u> | γὰρ | ὅτι τοῖς ἀγγέλοις αὐτοῦ <u>ἐντελεῖται</u> | περὶ σοῦ καὶ | ἐπὶ χειρῶν <u>ἀροῦσίν</u> σε, | μήποτε <u>προσκόψῃς</u> | πρὸς λίθον τὸν πόδα σου (D). ⁷<u>ἔφη</u> αὐτῷ ὁ Ἰησοῦς, πάλιν <u>γέγραπται</u>, οὐκ <u>ἐκπειράσεις</u> κύριον τὸν θεόν σου (D). ⁸<u>πάλιν</u> <u>παραλαμβάνει</u> αὐτὸν ὁ διάβολος | εἰς ὄρος ὑψηλὸν λίαν, | καὶ <u>δείκνυσιν</u> αὐτῷ πάσας τὰς βασιλείας τοῦ κόσμου | καὶ τὴν δόξαν αὐτῶν, ⁹καὶ <u>εἶπεν</u> αὐτῷ, ταῦτά σοι πάντα <u>δώσω</u> | ἐὰν πεσὼν <u>προσκυνήσῃς</u> μοι (D). ¹⁰τότε <u>λέγει</u> αὐτῷ ὁ Ἰησοῦς, <u>ὕπαγε</u>, Σατανᾶ· <u>γέγραπται</u> | γάρ, κύριον τὸν θεόν σου <u>προσκυνήσεις</u> | καὶ αὐτῷ μόνῳ <u>λατρεύσεις</u> (D). ¹¹τότε <u>ἀφίησιν</u> αὐτὸν ὁ διάβολος, | καὶ ἰδοὺ ἄγγελοι <u>προσῆλθον</u> | καὶ <u>διηκόνουν</u> αὐτῷ (D).

Philippians 1:3–11

³<u>εὐχαριστῶ</u> τῷ θεῷ μου | ἐπὶ πάσῃ τῇ μνείᾳ ὑμῶν, ⁴πάντοτε | ἐν πάσῃ δεήσει μου | ὑπὲρ πάντων ὑμῶν | μετὰ χαρᾶς τὴν δέησιν <u>ποιούμενος</u>, ⁵ | ἐπὶ τῇ κοινωνίᾳ ὑμῶν | εἰς τὸ εὐαγγέλιον | ἀπὸ τῆς πρώτης ἡμέρας | ἄχρι τοῦ νῦν, ⁶<u>πεποιθὼς</u> αὐτὸ τοῦτο, | ὅτι ὁ <u>ἐναρξάμενος</u> | ἐν ὑμῖν ἔργον ἀγαθὸν <u>ἐπιτελέσει</u> | ἄχρι ἡμέρας Χριστοῦ Ἰησοῦ (I) · ⁷ | καθώς <u>ἐστιν</u> δίκαιον ἐμοὶ τοῦτο <u>φρονεῖν</u> | ὑπὲρ πάντων ὑμῶν, | διὰ τὸ <u>ἔχειν</u> με | ἐν τῇ καρδίᾳ ὑμᾶς, | ἔν τε τοῖς δεσμοῖς μου | καὶ | ἐν τῇ ἀπολογίᾳ | καὶ βεβαιώσει τοῦ εὐαγγελίου συγκοινωνούς μου τῆς χάριτος πάντας ὑμᾶς <u>ὄντας</u> (D). ⁸μάρτυς | γάρ μου ὁ θεός, | ὡς <u>ἐπιποθῶ</u> πάντας ὑμᾶς | ἐν σπλάγχνοις Χριστοῦ Ἰησοῦ (D). ⁹ | καὶ τοῦτο προσεύχομαι, | ἵνα ἡ ἀγάπη ὑμῶν ἔτι μᾶλλον καὶ μᾶλλον <u>περισσεύῃ</u> | ἐν ἐπιγνώσει καὶ πάσῃ αἰσθήσει, ¹⁰ | εἰς τὸ <u>δοκιμάζειν</u> ὑμᾶς τὰ <u>διαφέροντα</u>, | ἵνα <u>ἦτε</u> εἰλικρινεῖς καὶ ἀπρόσκοποι | εἰς ἡμέραν Χριστοῦ, ¹¹<u>πεπληρωμένοι</u> καρπὸν δικαιοσύνης τὸν | διὰ Ἰησοῦ Χριστοῦ | εἰς δόξαν καὶ ἔπαινον θεοῦ (D).

Matthew 4:1–11 Paragraph Flow

¹τότε ὁ Ἰησοῦς <u>ἀνήχθη</u> {ΕΙΣ τὴν ἔρημον} ➜ {ΥΠΟ τοῦ πνεύματος},	INT
<u>πειρασθῆναι</u> {ΥΠΟ τοῦ διαβόλου}.	INF/purpose
↓ ²ΚΑΙ <u>νηστεύσας</u> ἡμέρας τεσσερά-➜ κοντα καὶ νύκτας τεσσεράκοντα,	PAR/time
ὕστερον <u>ἐπείνασεν</u>.	DEV/continuation
↓ ³ΚΑΙ <u>προσελθὼν</u>	PAR/time
ὁ <u>πειράζων</u> <u>εἶπεν</u> αὐτῷ,	DEV/intro. direct quote
ΕΙ υἱὸς <u>εἶ</u> τοῦ θεοῦ,	SUB/conditional
<u>εἰπὲ</u>	DEV/intro. indirect quote
ΙΝΑ οἱ λίθοι οὗτοι ἄρτοι <u>γένωνται</u>.	SUB/indirect quote
↓ ⁴ὁ ΔΕ <u>ἀποκριθεὶς</u>	PAR/time
<u>εἶπεν</u>,	DEV/intro. direct quote
<u>γέγραπται</u>,	DEV/intro. direct quote
οὐκ {ΕΠ᾽ ἄρτῳ μόνῳ} <u>ζήσεται</u> ➜ ὁ ἄνθρωπος, ΑΛΛ᾽ {ΕΠΙ παντὶ ῥήματι}	DEV/direct quote
<u>ἐκπορευομένῳ</u> {ΔΙΑ στόματος θεοῦ}.	PAR/adjective
⁵τότε <u>παραλαμβάνει</u> αὐτὸν ὁ διάβολος ➜ {ΕΙΣ τὴν ἁγίαν πόλιν},	DEV/continuation
ΚΑΙ <u>ἔστησεν</u> αυτον {ΕΠΙ τὸ πτερύγιον ➜ τοῦ ἱεροῦ},	DEV/continuation
⁶ΚΑΙ <u>λέγει</u> αὐτῷ,	DEV/intro. direct quote
ΕΙ υἱὸς <u>εἶ</u> τοῦ θεοῦ,	SUB/conditional
<u>βάλε</u> σεαυτὸν κάτω·	DEV/direct quote
<u>γέγραπται</u> ΓΑΡ	DEV/intro. direct quote
ΟΤΙ τοῖς ἀγγέλοις αὐτοῦ ➜ <u>ἐντελεῖται</u> {ΠΕΡΙ σοῦ}	SUB/direct quote
ΚΑΙ {ΕΠΙ χειρῶν} <u>ἀροῦσίν</u> σε,	SUB/direct quote

ΜΗΠΟΤΕ <u>προσκόψης</u> {ΠΡΟΣ λίθον} → τὸν πόδα σου.	SUB/neg. purpose
⁷<u>ἔφη</u> αὐτῷ ὁ Ἰησοῦς,	DEV/intro. direct quote
πάλιν <u>γέγραπται</u>,	DEV/intro. direct quote
οὐκ <u>ἐκπειράσεις</u> κύριον τὸν θεόν σου.	DEV/direct quote
⁸πάλιν <u>παραλαμβάνει</u> αὐτὸν ὁ διάβολος → {ΕΙΣ ὄρος ὑψηλὸν λίαν}	DEV/continuation
ΚΑΙ <u>δείκνυσιν</u> αὐτῷ πάσας τὰς βασιλείας → τοῦ κόσμου καὶ τὴν δόξαν αὐτῶν,	DEV/continuation
⁹καὶ <u>εἶπεν</u> αὐτῷ,	DEV/intro. direct quote
ταῦτά σοι πάντα <u>δώσω</u>	DEV/direct quote
ΕΑΝ . . . <u>προσκυνήσῃς</u> μοι.	SUB/conditional
<u>πεσὼν</u>	SUB/circumstance
¹⁰τότε <u>λέγει</u> αὐτῷ ὁ Ἰησοῦς,	DEV/intro. direct quote
<u>ὕπαγε</u>, Σατανᾶ·	DEV/direct quote
<u>γέγραπται</u> ΓΑΡ,	DEV/intro. direct quote
κύριον τὸν θεόν σου <u>προσκυνήσεις</u>	DEV/direct quote
ΚΑΙ αὐτῷ μόνῳ <u>λατρεύσεις</u>.	DEV/direct quote
¹¹τότε <u>ἀφίησιν</u> αὐτὸν ὁ διάβολος,	DEV/continuation
καὶ ἰδοὺ ἄγγελοι <u>προσῆλθον</u>	DEV/continuation
καὶ <u>διηκόνουν</u> αὐτῷ.	DEV/continuation

1. Preliminary paragraph summary.

Jesus was tempted by the devil three times, and every time He triumphed over the tempter by referring to the Word of God.

2. Important verbs.

ἀνήχθη ("was led")—main verb of the introductory sentence
πειρασθῆναι ("to be tempted")—difference between test and tempt?
ζήσεται ("shall live")—quality of living? eternal life?

γέγραπται ("it is written")—note perfect tense
προσκυνήσεις ("you shall worship")—what exactly is worship?

3. Important structure markers.

εἰ ("if")—what kind of condition is implied by this?
μήποτε ("lest")—a kind of subordinate conjunction; negative
ἐάν ("if")—what kind of condition is implied by this?

4. Important patterns.

"It is written" four times—very important. Emphasizes God's Word.

"If you are God's Son"—two times. Was Satan assuming Jesus to be God's Son or trying to get Him to doubt His sonship?

"Worship"—two times. How important is worship?

Note geographical moves: desert to holy city to high mountain. Does this constitute a pattern?

5. Preliminary application/relevance

Although the focus of Matthew is to record a real event in the life of Jesus, the application might be that Satan tempts believers today in the same ways that he tempted Jesus. Jesus' key to victory was the Word of God. It is still the key.

Philippians 1:3–11 Paragraph Flow

³ <u>Εὐχαριστῶ</u> τῷ θεῷ μου {ΕΠΙ πάσῃ ➜ τῇ μνείᾳ ὑμῶν}	INT
⁴πάντοτε {ΕΝ πάσῃ δεήσει μου} ➜ {ΥΠΕΡ πάντων ὑμῶν} {ΜΕΤΑ ➜ χαρᾶς} τὴν δέησιν <u>ποιούμενος</u>, ➜ ⁵{ΕΠΙ τῇ κοινωνίᾳ ὑμῶν} {ΕΙΣ ➜ τὸ εὐαγγέλιον} {ΑΠΟ τῆς ➜ πρώτης ἡμέρας} {ΑΧΡΙ τοῦ νῦν},	PAR/time
<u>πεποιθὼς</u> αὐτὸ τοῦτο,	PAR/cause
⁶ΟΤΙ ὁ <u>ἐναρξάμενος</u> {ΕΝ ὑμῖν ➜ ἔργον ἀγαθὸν} <u>ἐπιτελέσει</u> {ΑΧΡΙ ➜ ἡμέρας Χριστοῦ Ἰησοῦ}·	SUB/content
⁷ ΚΑΘΩΣ <u>ἐστιν</u> δίκαιον ἐμοὶ ➜ τοῦτο <u>φρονεῖν</u> {ΥΠΕΡ πάντων ὑμῶν}	SUB/comparison
ΔΙΑ ΤΟ <u>ἔχειν</u> με {ΕΝ τῇ καρδίᾳ ὑμᾶς},	INF/cause
{ΕΝ τε τοῖς δεσμοῖς μου} καὶ ➜ {ΕΝ τῇ ἀπολογίᾳ καὶ βεβαιώσει ➜ τοῦ εὐαγγελίου} συγκοινωνούς ➜ μου τῆς χάριτος πάντας ὑμᾶς <u>ὄντας</u>.	PAR/cause
⁸ μάρτυς ΓΑΡ μου ὁ θεός	DEV/cause
ΩΣ <u>ἐπιποθῶ</u> πάντας ὑμᾶς {ΕΝ ➜ σπλάγχνοις Χριστοῦ Ἰησοῦ}.	SUB/content
⁹ ΚΑΙ τοῦτο <u>προσεύχομαι</u>,	DEV/continuation
ΙΝΑ ἡ ἀγάπη ὑμῶν ἔτι μᾶλλον ➜ καὶ μᾶλλον <u>περισσεύῃ</u> {ΕΝ ➜ ἐπιγνώσει καὶ πάσῃ αἰσθήσει}	SUB/indirect quote
¹⁰ ΕΙΣ ΤΟ <u>δοκιμάζειν</u> ὑμᾶς ➜ τὰ <u>διαφέροντα</u>,	INF/result
ΙΝΑ <u>ἦτε</u> εἰλικρινεῖς καὶ ➜ ἀπρόσκοποι {ΕΙΣ ἡμέραν Χριστοῦ},	SUB/purpose
¹¹ <u>πεπληρωμένοι</u> καρπὸν ➜ δικαιοσύνης τὸν {ΔΙΑ Ἰησοῦ ➜ Χριστοῦ} {ΕΙΣ δόξαν καὶ ➜ ἔπαινον θεοῦ}.	PAR/result

1. Preliminary paragraph summary.

Paul prayed for his dear Philippian friends to keep growing in their love, confident that God's work in them would reach a wonderful completion at the time of the "day of Christ."

2. Important verbs.

εὐχαριστῶ ("I thank")—main verb of the introductory sentence
ἐπιτελέσει ("he will complete")—future tense
ἐπιποθῶ ("I long for")—note the intensity of Paul's feeling
δοκιμάζειν ("to approve")—word seems to have several meanings
πεπληρωμένοι ("filled")—note perfect tense

3. Important structure markers.

διὰ τό ("because")—introduces infinitive of cause
εἰς τό ("so that")—introduces infinitive of result (or purpose?)
ἵνα ("that")—used twice, apparently with two difference senses

4. Important patterns.

Words for prayer are prominent: εὐχαριστῶ, δεήσει, προσεύχομαι. Is there a real difference among them?
"Christ"—four times. Christ is the center of everything for Paul.
"God"—three times. The paragraph begins and ends with God.
"Day of Christ"—two times. Paul lived in light of the coming day of Christ.
Prepositions vary widely: ἐπί, ἐν, ὑπέρ, μετά, εἰς, ἀπό, ἄχρι, διά. There doesn't seem to be any particular pattern.
"Began" vs. "will complete"—an interesting contrast.

5. Preliminary application/relevance

Paul's prayer for the Philippians shows what today's Christians should be striving for. A message on this text should perhaps focus more on Christian growth than on "how to pray like an apostle."

Chapter 3

The five verb forms I think are the most interesting in each text from the perspective of tense are underlined.

Matthew 4
Verse 1: ἀνήχθη—simple, no
πειρασθῆναι—unspecified, no

Verse 2: νηστεύσας—unspecified, no
ἐπείνασεν—simple, no
Verse 3: προσελθὼν—simple, no
πειράζων—process, no
εἶπεν—simple, no
εἶ—descriptive, no
εἰπέ—unspecified, no
γένωνται—unspecified, no
Verse 4: ἀποκριθείς—unspecified, no
εἶπεν—simple, no
γέγραπται—pure, yes
ζήσεται—imperative, yes
ἐκπορευομένῳ—process, no
Verse 5: παραλαμβάνει—historical, no
ἔστησεν—simple, no
Verse 6: λέγει—historical, no
εἶ—descriptive, no
βάλε—unspecified, no
γέγραπται—pure, yes
ἐντελεῖται—predictive, no
ἀροῦσίν—predictive, no
προσκόψῃς—descriptive, no
Verse 7: ἔφη—simple, no
γέγραπται—pure, yes
ἐκπειράσεις—predictive, no
Verse 8: παραλαμβάνει—historical, no
δείκνυσιν—historical, no
Verse 9: εἶπεν—simple, no
δώσω—predictive, yes
πεσὼν—unspecified, no
προσκυνήσῃς—predictive, no
Verse 10: λέγει—historical, no
ὕπαγε—process, no
γέγραπται—pure, yes
προσκυνήσεις—imperative, yes
λατρεύσεις—imperative, yes
Verse 11: ἀφίησιν—historical, no
προσῆλθον—simple, no
διηκόνουν—simple, no

Philippians 1

Verse 3: εὐχαριστῶ—descriptive (iterative), yes
Verse 4: ποιούμενος—process, yes
Verse 6: πεποιθὼς—pure, yes
ἐναρξάμενος—unspecified, no
ἐπιτελέσει—predictive, yes
Verse 7: ἐστιν—descriptive, no
φρονεῖν—process, no
ἔχειν—process, no
ὄντας—process, no
Verse 8: ἐπιποθῶ—descriptive, yes
Verse 9: προσεύχομαι—descriptive (iterative), yes
περισσεύῃ—process, yes
Verse 10: δοκιμάζειν—process, yes
διαφέροντα—process, no
ἦτε—descriptive, no
Verse 11: πεπληρωμένοι—pure, yes

Chapter 4

The five verb forms I think are the most interesting in each text
from a mood persepective are underlined.

Matthew 4

Verse 1: ἀνήχθη—statement, no
πειρασθῆναι—purpose, yes
Verse 2: νηστεύσας—circumstantial (time), no
ἐπείνασεν—statement, no
Verse 3: προσελθὼν—circumstantial (time), no
πειράζων—noun element, no
εἶπεν—statement, no
εἰ—conditional, yes
εἰπέ—command, no
γένωνται—content (indirect quotation), no
Verse 4: ἀποκριθεὶς—circumstantial (time), no
εἶπεν—statement, no
γέγραπται—statement, no
ζήσεται—predictive, no
ἐκπορευομένῳ—adjective, no
Verse 5: παραλαμβάνει—statement, no
ἔστησεν—statement, no

Verse 6: λέγει—statement, no
εἰ—conditional, yes
βάλε—command, no
γέγραπται—statement, no
ἐντελεῖται—predictive, no
ἀροῦσίν—predictive, no
προσκόψῃς—purpose, no
Verse 7: ἔφη—statement, no
γέγραπται—statement, no
ἐκπειράσεις—predictive, no
Verse 8: παραλαμβάνει—statement, no
δείκνυσιν—statement, no
Verse 9: εἶπεν—statement, no
δώσω—predictive, no
πεσὼν—circumstantial (manner), no
προσκυνήσῃς—conditional, no
Verse 10: λέγει—statement, no
ὕπαγε—command, yes
γέγραπται—statement, no
πρυσκυνήσεις—imperative, yes
λατρεύσεις—imperative, yes
Verse 11: ἀφίησιν—statement, no
προσῆλθον—statement, no
διηκόνουν—statement, no

Philippians 1

Verse 3: εὐχαριστῶ—statement, yes
Verse 4: ποιούμενος—circumstantial (time), no
Verse 6: πεποιθὼς—circumstantial (cause), yes
ἐναρξάμενος—noun element, no
ἐπιτελέσει—statement, no
Verse 7: ἐστιν—statement, yes
φρονεῖν—noun element, no
ἔχειν—cause, yes
ὄντας—circumstantial (cause), yes
Verse 8: ἐπιποθῶ—statement, no
Verse 9: προσεύχομαι—statement, no
περισσεύῃ—statement, no
Verse 10: δοκιμάζειν—content, no
διαφέροντα—noun element, no
ἦτε—result, yes

Verse 11: πεπληρωμένοι—circumstantial (result), yes

Chapter 5

Matthew 4

The five genitive forms I think are the most interesting are underlined.

Verse 1: τοῦ πνεύματος—agent (object of preposition), yes
τοῦ διαβόλου—agent (object of preposition), yes
Verse 3: τοῦ θεοῦ—relationship, yes
Verse 4: στόματος—object of preposition, no
θεοῦ—possession, no
Verse 5: τοῦ ἱεροῦ—possession, no
Verse 6: τοῦ θεοῦ—relationship, no
αὐτοῦ—possession, no
σοῦ—object of preposition, no
χειρῶν—object of preposition, yes
σοῦ—object of preposition, no
Verse 7: σου—relationship, no
Verse 8: τοῦ κόσμου—content or adjective, yes
αὐτῶν—possession, no
Verse 10: σου—relationship, no

Philippians 1

Verse 3: μου—relationship, no
ὑμῶν—objective, no
Verse 4: μου—possession, no
πάντων ὑμῶν—object of preposition, no
χαρᾶς—object of preposition, no
Verse 5: ὑμῶν—possession, no
τῆς πρώτης ἡμέρας—object of preposition, yes
τοῦ νῦν—object of preposition, no
Verse 6: ἡμέρας—object of preposition, yes
Χριστοῦ Ἰησοῦ—source or possession, yes
Verse 7: πάντων ὑμῶν—object of preposition, no
μου—relationship, no
τοῦ εὐαγγελίου—objective, yes
μου—relationship, no
τῆς χάριτος—objective, no
Verse 8: μου—relationship, no

Χριστοῦ Ἰησοῦ—source, no
Verse 9: ὑμῶν—relationship, no
Verse 10: Χριστοῦ—source or possession, no
Verse 11: <u>δικαιοσύνης</u>—appositive, yes
Ἰησοῦ Χριστοῦ—object of preposition, no
θεοῦ —objective, no

Chapter 6

Review the answer key for chapter 2 for the first part of the exercise.

Narrative questions about Matthew 4:1–11.

1. Setting: The wilderness, immediately following Jesus' baptism.

2. Subject: Jesus

3. Object: No object

4. Opponent: The devil

5. Dialogue: The narrative is filled with direct quotations. The dialogue begins with the devil and moves to Jesus. This cycle happens three times, with Jesus having the last word.

6. Character development: The evil nature of Satan is seen. Jesus is recognized as the one who can completely defeat the tempter.

7. Conflict resolution: The account resolves in verse 11, with Jesus being attended by the angels.

8. Emotional tone: Extreme conflict.

9. Narrator's presence: Nobody knows how Matthew got this information. Perhaps Jesus later told the apostles about this event. The narrator also does not tell us how Jesus and the devil moved from the wilderness to the holy city to a high mountain. This raises the question of whether this might have occurred in a visionary form.

10. Contrasts: Jesus vs. the devil; obeying God vs. disobeying; quoting Scripture fairly (v. 7) vs. misquoting Scripture (v. 6); physical needs (bread) vs. spiritual needs (word of God).

11. Climax: The climax is seen at verse 10. The name "Satan" is used for the first time. The tempter is unmasked and forced to flee; Jesus is the victor.

12. Summary: The narrative focus helps one realize that this was a real, historical event, a titanic struggle. Here is the classic presentation of good vs. evil. Perhaps in a sermon on this text drama could be employed.

Composition questions about Philippians 1:3–11.

Comparison or contrast: Paul explicitly compares the rightness of God's completing His work in the Philippians with the rightness of His feelings for them, using κάθως.

Repetition: Christ Jesus (three times), God (twice), day of Christ (twice).

Continuity: None observed

Climax: "To the glory and praise of God" (v. 11)

Cruciality: None observed

Interchange: None observed

Particularization: None observed

Generalization: None observed

Cause to Effect (Result): "So that you will approve the things that differ" (v. 10); "So that you will be filled with the fruit of righteousness" (v. 11).

Substantiation: "Because I have you in my heart" (v. 7); "because you are partakers. . ." (v. 7).

Progression: None observed

Radiation: None observed

Word patterns in Matthew 4:1–11 and Philippians 1:3–11.

Matthew 4:1–11

Synonym Patterns: Several different words for "said" are found. These seem to be used for variety.

Semantic Fields: No special patterns observed

Antonyms: None observed

Cognates: Tempt/tempter

Alliteration: None observed

Chiasm: None observed

Summary of your study of word patterns: This text has no particularly striking patterns of words.

Philippians 1:3–11

Synonym Patterns: Several words of overlapping relations for prayer are used: εὐχαριστῶ, δεήσει, προσεύχομαι.

Semantic Fields: Words for prayer are prominent as noted above.

Antonyms: None observed.

Cognates: None observed

Alliteration: None observed

Chiasm: None observed

Summary of your study of word patterns. The only interesting material on word patterns are the various words for prayer, which deserve mention in a sermon.

Appendix

Summary of Verb Tense

1. AORIST

SIMPLE (or UNSPECIFIED or CONSTATIVE)	=	indicative main use
PROVERBIAL (or GNOMIC)	=	indicative special use
FUTURISTIC	=	indicative special use
LITERARY (or EPISTOLARY)	=	indicative special use
UNSPECIFIED (or SIMPLE)	=	non-indicative use
SUBJUNCTIVE plus μή or οὐ μή	=	non-indicative special use

2. PRESENT

DESCRIPTIVE (subcategories: CONTINUOUS, ITERATIVE, PUNCTILIAR)	=	indicative main use
HISTORICAL	=	indicative special use
PROVERBIAL (or GNOMIC)	=	indicative special use

FUTURISTIC (subcategory: CONATIVE)	=	indicative special use
PROCESS	=	non-indicative use
IMPERATIVE plus μή	=	non-indicative special use

3. PERFECT

PURE (or CONSUMMATIVE)	=	indicative main use
INTENSIVE	=	indicative special use
HISTORICAL	=	indicative special use
PURE (or CONSUMMATIVE)	=	non-indicative use

4. FUTURE

PREDICTIVE (or PROPHETIC)	=	indicative main use
PROVERBIAL (or GNOMIC or APHORISTIC)	=	indicative special use
IMPERATIVE (or VOLITIONAL)	=	indicative special use
PERFECT	=	indicative special use
PURPOSE	=	non-indicative use

5. IMPERFECT

DESCRIPTIVE (subcategory: ITERATIVE)	=	indicative main use
INCEPTIVE	=	indicative special use
INFERENTIAL	=	indicative special use

6. PLUPERFECT

| PURE (or CONSUMMATIVE) | = | indicative main use |
| INTENSIVE | = | indicative special use |

Summary of Mood Syntax

1. INDICATIVE

STATEMENT	=	main use
INTERROGATIVE	=	special use
COMMAND FUTURE	=	special use
CONDITIONAL (first class or second class)	=	special use

2. SUBJUNCTIVE

EXHORTATION (or HORTATORY or COHORATIVE)	=	main verb use
PROHIBITION (aorist tense)	=	main verb use
DENIAL (or EMPHATIC NEGATION)	=	main verb use
DELIBERATION	=	main verb use
PURPOSE (or FINAL)	=	dependent verb use
RESULT (or CONSECUTIVE)	=	dependent verb use
CONTENT (includes INDIRECT QUOTATION)	=	dependent verb use
CONDITIONAL (third class)	=	dependent verb use
INDEFINITE (-ever translation)	=	dependent verb use

3. OPTATIVE

VOLITIONAL	=	main use
CURSE (or IMPRECATION)	=	special use
DELIBERATION	=	special use

4. IMPERATIVE

COMMAND	=	main use
PROHIBITION (present tense)	=	special use
PERMISSION (third person)	=	special use
REQUEST (or ENTREATY)	=	special use
CONDITIONAL	=	special use

5. INFINITIVE

NOUN ELEMENT (SUBSTANTIVE)		
NOUN OR ADJECTIVE COMPLEMENT		
VERB PHRASE (includes INDIRECT QUOTATION)		
PURPOSE (or FINAL)	=	adverbial use
RESULT (or CONSECUTIVE)	=	adverbial use
CAUSE (or CAUSAL)	=	adverbial use
TIME (or TEMPORAL)	=	adverbial use
INDEPENDENT	=	unexpected use

6. PARTICIPLE

ADJECTIVE (includes SUBJECT COMPLEMENT and OBJECT COMPLEMENT)		
NOUN ELEMENT (SUBSTANTIVE)		
CIRCUMSTANTIAL (TIME, PURPOSE, RESULT, CAUSE, CONDITION, CONCESSION, MEANS, or MANNER)	=	adverbial use
VERB PHRASE (incl. PERIPHRASTIC)	=	dependent verb use
INDEPENDENT VERB (includes UNRESTRICTED)	=	main verb use

Summary of the Genitive

1. DESCRIBING A NOUN

POSSESSIVE OR RELATIONAL	
possessive genitive	δοῦλοι Χριστοῦ
relational genitive	μήτηρ αὐτοῦ
SOURCE OR SUBJECTIVE	
source genitive (ablative of source)	σοφίαν τοῦ κόσμου
subjective genitive	τὸ βάπτισμα Ἰωάννου
OBJECTIVE	
objective genitive	μαρτύριον τοῦ Χριστοῦ
APPOSITIVE OR CONTENT	
appositive genitive (epexegetic/identity)	μέρη τῆς γῆς
content genitive	δίκτυον τῶν ἰχθύων
PARTITIVE	
partitive genitive (ablative of the whole)	πτωχοὺς τῶν ἁγίων
SEPARATION OR COMPARATIVE	
separation genitive (ablative of separation)	ξένοι τῶν διαθηκῶν
comparative genitive (ablative of comparison)	πολλῶν στρουθίων διαφέρετε ὑμεῖς
ADJECTIVE	
adjective genitive (descriptive, attributive)	μαμωνᾶ τῆς ἀδικίας

2. DESCRIBING A VERB

TIME OR PLACE	ἵνα βάψῃ τὸ ἄκρον τοῦ δακτύλου αὐτοῦ ὕδατος
AGENT (ablative of agent)	τὸ ἔλαττον ὑπὸ τοῦ κρείττονος εὐλογεῖται

DIRECT OBJECT	
verbs of perceiving or sensing	ἀκούει ἡμῶν
verbs of touching or taking hold of	ἐπιλαβόμενος τῆς χειρὸς
verbs of sharing in or eating	τραπέζης κυρίου μετέχειν
verbs of taking charge or ruling	κυριεύουσιν αὐτῶν
verbs of remembering	μιμνήσκεσθε τῶν δεσμίων
verbs of desiring or despising	καλοῦ ἔργου ἐπιθυμει
verbs of departing, removing, ceasing, abstaining, missing, or lacking (ablative)	λείπεται σοφίας
GENITIVE ABSOLUTE	ἀναχωρησάντων δὲ αὐτῶν ἰδοὺ ἄγγελος κυρίου φαίνεται

3. DESCRIBING AN ADJECTIVE

genitive of reference	μεστὸν ἰχθύων

4. FOLLOWING A PREPOSITION

object of a formal preposition	ὑπὲρ τῶν ἀδελφῶν
object of an informal preposition	χωρὶς τῶν ἔργων

Glossary and Subject Index

ABLATIVE OF AGENT: same as agent genitive (5.2.2.)

ABLATIVE OF COMPARISON: same as comparative genitive (5.1.6.)

ABLATIVE OF SEPARATION: same as separation genitive (5.1.6.)

ABLATIVE OF SOURCE: same as source genitive (5.1.2.)

ABLATIVE OF THE WHOLE: same as partitive genitive (5.1.5.)

ACCUSATIVE OF GENERAL REFERENCE: an accusative noun or pronoun that indicates who is doing the action (= the subject) of an infinitive (4.5.4.3.)

ACTION NOUN: a noun that necessarily implies some activity (5.1.2.)

ADJECTIVE COMPLEMENT INFINITIVE: an infinitive that completes the meaning of an adjective (4.5.2.)

ADJECTIVE GENITIVE: a genitive form telling some quality or attribute of the noun modified (5.1.7.)

ADJECTIVE: a word that describes a noun (1.1.2.2.)

ADVERB: a word that describes a verb (1.1.2.1.)

ADVERSATIVE CLAUSE: same as concession clause (4.6.3.6.)

AGENT GENITIVE: a genitive noun or pronoun used to identify the person responsible (= agent) for the action of a passive verb; the genitive noun follows ὑπό or διά (5.2.2.)

ALLITERATION: a word that begins with the same speech sound as some other word (6.4.5.)

ALPHA PRIVATIVE: an alpha prefixed to a Greek word making it negative (4.7.)

155

ANTECEDENT ACTION: action that happens in time before some other action (4.5.4.4.)

ANTECEDENT: the noun referred to by a pronoun (1.1.2.2.)

ANTONYM: a word that is opposite or contrasts in one way or another to some other word; negatives/positives are a common kind of antonym (6.4.3.)

AORIST TENSE: the most common Greek tense; carries no meaning in itself (3.1 and following subsections)

APHORISTIC FUTURE: same as proverbial future (3.4.2.1.)

APODOSIS (uh-POD-uh-sis): the *then* (= main) part of a conditional sentence (4.1.2.3, 4.2.2.4; 4.4.2.4; 4.6.3.5; 4.7.1; 4.7.1–3.)

APPOSITIVE GENITIVE: a genitive noun that renames the noun modified (5.1.4.)

ARTICLE: in English, *a, an, or the*; in Greek, all forms of ὁ (1.1.2.2.)

ASYNDETON (uh-SIN-duh-tuhn): beginning a sentence without any coordinate conjunction (1.3.2.)

ATTENDANT CIRCUMSTANCE PARTICIPLE OR CLAUSE: same as independent participle or clause (4.6.5.)

ATTRIBUTIVE GENITIVE: same as adjective genitive (5.1.7.)

ATTRIBUTIVE PARTICIPLE: a participle that describes a noun (4.6.1.)

"BE" VERB: a verb expressing a condition or a state of being (1.2.3.4.)

CAUSE PARTICIPLE: (= causal) (circumstantial) used in a dependent clause that tells the cause of the action in the main clause (4.6.3.4.)

CAUSE INFINITIVE: (= causal) used in a dependent clause to tell the cause of the action in the main clause (4.5.4.3.)

CAUSE TO EFFECT: the compositional pattern of stating an action and then the result(s) of that action (6.3.9.)

CHIASM (KAI-az-um): a literary pattern in which, in a series of four elements, elements one and four are alike and elements two and three are alike; sometimes referred to as the *a-b-b-a* pattern (6.4.6.)

CIRCUMSTANTIAL PARTICIPLE: a participle describing another verb within a sentence (= adverbial usage), usually describing the main verb of the sentence; includes time, purpose, result cause, condition, concession, means, and manner participles (4.6.3.)

CLIMAX: the logical or narrative high point of a didactic argument or a narrative account (6.2.1; 6.3.4.)

COGNATE: a word that shares the same original language root as some other word (6.4.4.)

COHORTATIVE SUBJUNCTIVE: same as exhortation subjunctive (4.2.1.1.)

COMMAND FUTURE INDICATIVE: in the indicative mood, a second person future form that expresses a command rather than a prediction (3.4.2.2; 4.1.2.2.)

COMMAND IMPERATIVE: use of the imperative mood to issue an order by one with authority so to speak; main use of the imperative (4.4.1.)

COMPARATIVE GENITIVE: a genitive noun indicating what the noun modified is compared to or different than; requires English *than* in translation (5.1.6.)

COMPARISON: a compositional pattern that shows how two items are alike (2.4.3; 6.3.1.)

COMPLEX SENTENCE: a sentence with only one main clause and at least one dependent clause (1.2.1.3.)

COMPOSITIONAL PATTERN: the literary shape of a paragraph (or paragraphs) of writing; discovered by seeking answers to certain literary questions; usually applied to non-narrative or didactic material (6.3.)

COMPOUND SENTENCE: any sentence with more than one main clause and no dependent clauses (1.2.1.1.)

COMPOUND WORD: a word with two stems pushed together (1.1.3.)

COMPOUND-COMPLEX SENTENCE: a sentence with more than one main clause and at least one dependent clause (1.2.1.3.)

CONATIVE PRESENT: in the indicative mood a present tense verb that tells of an attempted or intended action; a kind of futuristic present (3.2.2.3.)

CONCESSION PARTICIPLE OR CLAUSE: (circumstantial) used to express a circumstance adversative to the action in the main clause; the main action is accomplished in spite of the other action (4.6.3.6.)

CONDITION PARTICIPLE: (circumstantial) used in a dependent clause that tells a condition upon which the action in the main clause depends (4.6.3.5.)

CONDITIONAL CLAUSE: a clause stating *if* in some way; technically called the protasis (4.1.2.3, 4.2.2.4; 4.4.2.4; 4.6.3.5; 4.7.3.1; 4.7.1-3.)

CONDITIONAL IMPERATIVE: a specialized use of a Greek imperative mood to imply *if* (4.4.2.4.)

CONDITIONAL INDICATIVE: use of the indicative mood in first class conditions to assume a condition was true or in second class conditions to assume a condition was false (3.5.2.2; 4.1.2.3.)

CONDITIONAL SUBJUNCTIVE: use of the subjunctive mood in third class conditions to indicate an action that might or might not be fulfilled (4.2.2.4.)

CONNOTATION: in word study, a specialized, often emotion-oriented meaning that a word acquires for some but not all speakers of a language (6.5.6.)

CONSECUTIVE PARTICIPLE, INFINITIVE, OR SUBJUNCTIVE: (circumstantial) same as result participle, infinitive or subjunctive (4.2.2.2; 4.5.4.2; 4.6.3.3.)

CONSTATIVE AORIST: same as simple aorist (3.1.1.)

CONSUMMATIVE PERFECT: same as pure perfect (3.3.1.)

CONTEMPORANEOUS ACTION: same as simultaneous action (4.5.4.4.)

CONTENT GENITIVE: a genitive noun that names the contents or that which fills the noun modified (5.1.4.)

CONTENT SUBJUNCTIVE: a dependent clause with a subjunctive verb, often following ἵνα, that gives the content of a wish command, thought, or indirect quotation (4.2.2.3; 4.7.3.2.)

CONTIGUOUS RELATIONS: in word study, words that belong to the same semantic field but are not used interchangeably; for example, in English, *humming* and *whistling* (6.5.5.)

CONTINUITY: a compositional pattern that continues an author's theme without repetition (6.3.3.)

CONTINUOUS PRESENT: in the indicative a present tense verb that tells of an action in progress without ceasing at the present time; a kind of descriptive present (3.2.1.)

CONTRAST: a narrative pattern in which elements such as good/evil or life/death are put side by side; a compositional pattern that shows how two such items are different (2.4.3; 6.2.1; 6.3.1.)

COORDINATE CIRCUMSTANCE PARTICIPLE OR CLAUSE: same as independent participle or clause (4.6.5; 5.2.4.3.)

COORDINATE CONJUNCTION: a word that joins paragraphs, sentences, verbs, or grammatical equals within a sentence, for example καί (1.1.2.1; 2.2.3.3.)

CRUCIALITY: the turning point of a narrative or argument (6.3.5.)

CURSE OPTATIVE: use of the optative mood to wish harm on someone or something (4.3.2.1.)

DATIVE OF ADVANTAGE: a dative noun or pronoun that tells for whom the action of a verb is done in a sentence without a direct object (1.2.2.4.)

DELIBERATION OPTATIVE OR SUBJUNCTIVE: use of the optative or subjunctive mood to ask a question out of perplexity or hesitancy (4.2.1.4; 4.3.2.2.)

DENIAL SUBJUNCTIVE: use of a second person aorist subjunctive with οὐ μή to assert strongly that an action can never happen (4.2.1.3.)

DENOTATION: in word study, the meaning(s) of a word for all native speakers (6.5.6.)

DEPENDENT CLAUSE: a group of words that cannot stand alone grammatically and that usually contains a verb (1.2.1.3.)

DESCRIPTIVE GENITIVE: same as adjective genitive (5.1.7.)

DESCRIPTIVE IMPERFECT: in the indicative mood an imperfect verb that tells of an action in progress in the past time; the main usage of the imperfect (3.5.1.)

DESCRIPTIVE PRESENT: in the indicative mood, a present tense verb that tells of an action in progress at the present time; the main usage of the present (3.2.1.)

DEVELOPMENT SENTENCE: a sentence in a paragraph that logically expands the theme or introductory sentence of a paragraph (1.3.2.)

DIACHRONIC WORD STUDY: study of a word's usage throughout a long period of time (6.5.1.)

DIRECT OBJECT: the recipient of the action done by the subject of a sentence (1.2.2.3.)

DIRECT OBJECT GENITIVE (or ablative): a genitive (or ablative) noun or pronoun serving as the direct object for certain Greek verbs (5.2.3.)

DIRECT QUOTATION: a record of the exact words of a speaker or writing (4.7.3.1.)

DISCOURSE ANALYSIS: same as macrostructure analysis; note particularly the Discourse Segmentation Apparatus in the fourth edition of the UBS *Greek New Testament* (6 introduction)

EMPHATIC NEGATION SUBJUNCTIVE: same as denial subjunctive (4.2.1.3.)

ENTREATY IMPERATIVE: same as request imperative (4.4.2.3.)

EPEXEGETIC GENITIVE: same as appositive genitive (5.1.4.)

EPISTOLARY AORIST: same as literary aorist (3.1.2.3.)

ETYMOLOGY: study of a word's history and component parts (6.5.1.)

EXHORTATION SUBJUNCTIVE: use of the first person plural subjunctive to encourage others to join in an action; usually involves an English translation *let us* ___ (4.2.1.1.)

FINAL PARTICIPLE, INFINITIVE, OR SUBJUNCTIVE: same as purpose participle, infinitive, or subjunctive (4.2.2.1; 4.5.4.1; 4.6.3.2.)

FORMAL PREPOSITION: one of 17 Greek words that can function only as a preposition (2.2.3.1; 6.4.)

FUNCTIONAL PREPOSITION: one of several Greek words that serve both informally as a preposition (with a genitive noun following) as well as in some other grammatical way (2.2.3.1; 5.4.)

FUTURE PERFECT TENSE: a rare Greek tense indicating action that will be completed in the future (3.4.2.3.)

FUTURE TENSE: a Greek tense that emphasizes future time (3.4 and following subsections)

FUTURISTIC AORIST: in the indicative mood an aorist verb that tells a future action (3.1.2.2.)

FUTURISTIC PRESENT: in the indicative mood a present tense verb that tells a future action (3.2.2.3.)

GENERALIZATION: the compositional pattern of giving specific examples or illustrations and then giving a general principle (6.3.8.)

GENITIVE ABSOLUTE: a clause containing noun or pronoun in the genitive along with a genitive participle of the same gender and number that serves as an adverb modifier to a main clause; the genitive noun or pronoun serves as the subject of the action of the participle (5.2.4.)

GENITIVE OF IDENTITY: same as appositive genitive (5.1.4.)

GENITIVE OF REFERENCE: a genitive modifying an adjective (5.3.)

GNOMIC PRESENT, FUTURE, OR AORIST: same as proverbial present, future, or aorist (3.1.2.1; 3.2.2.2; 3.4.2.1.)

HISTORICAL PERFECT: in the indicative mood a perfect tense verb that tells vividly of a past action (3.3.2.2.)

HISTORICAL PRESENT: in the indicative mood a present tense verb that tells vividly of a past action (3.2.2.1.)

HORTATORY SUBJUNCTIVE: same as exhortation subjunctive (4.2.1.1.)

IDENTITY GENITIVE: same as appositive genitive (5.1.4.)

IDIOM: a phrase or clause that means something other than the sum of its parts (6.5.7.)

IMPERATIVE MOOD: the mood that indicates the intention of the action if the speaker or writer's will prevails (4.4.)

IMPERFECT TENSE: a Greek tense that carries the idea of action over a period of past time (3.5 and following subsections)

IMPRECATION OPTATIVE: same as curse optative (4.3.2.1.)

INCEPTIVE IMPERFECT: in the indicative mood an imperfect verb that tells of the beginning of an action in the past (3.5.2.1.)

INCLUSIVE RELATIONS: in word study, when the meaning of one word includes the meaning of another word; for example in English, *clothes* includes *jacket* (6.5.5.)

INDEFINITE SUBJUNCTIVE: a subjunctive verb in a dependent clause in which the subject is uncertain or indefinite; in Greek uses ἄν; in English translation employs *-ever* (4.2.2.5.)

INDEPENDENT INFINITIVE OR PARTICIPLE: a participle or infinitive functioning as the main verb (4.5.4.5; 4.6.5.)

INDICATIVE MOOD: the normal mood for speech and writing that indicates the action of the verb is actual rather than potential (4.1.)

INDIRECT OBJECT: tells who or what receives the direct object of a sentence (1.2.2.4.)

INDIRECT QUOTATION: a clause giving the substance of a speaker's words or writing without using his or her exact words (4.2.2.3; 4.7.3.2.)

INFERENTIAL IMPERFECT: in the indicative mood the imperfect tense used in second class conditions to bring up situations in which something could have happened but did not (3.5.2.2.)

INFINITIVE: in Greek, a word that is part verb and part noun; considered a near mood or partial mood

INTENSIVE PERFECT: a perfect tense verb emphasizing existing results and translated as an English present; especially includes forms of οἶδα (3.3.2.1.)

INTENSIVE PLUPERFECT: a pluperfect verb emphasizing existing results and translated as an English past; especially includes forms of οἶδα (3.6.2.)

INTERCHANGE: a narrative or compositional pattern of going back and forth between one subject and another (6.3.6.)

INTERROGATIVE INDICATIVE: the use of the indicative mood in a question; usually in a request for factual information (4.1.2.1.)

INTRANSITIVE VERB: any verb in a sentence whose meaning is so complete that no direct object is required (1.2.3.2.)

INTRODUCTORY SENTENCE: a sentence in a paragraph that announces the paragraph theme (1.3.2.)

ITERATIVE IMPERFECT: in the indicative mood an imperfect verb that tells of an action repeated in the past time; a kind of descriptive imperfect (3.5.1.)

ITERATIVE PRESENT: in the indicative mood a present tense verb that tells of an action repeated at the present time; a kind of descriptive present (3.2.1.)

LEXICAL ENTRY: the dictionary form of a word (1.1.1.)

LITERARY AORIST: in the indicative mood use of an aorist verb that tells of an action which is past from a reader's perspective but present from a writer's perspective (3.1.2.3.)

MACROSTRUCTURE: analysis of patterns in a particular speech or writing that consider relationships beyond the sentence level (6.1 introduction)

MAIN CLAUSE: a group of words that can stand alone and that contains a verb or an implied verb (1.2.1.1; 6.1 introduction)

MANNER (CIRCUMSTANTIAL) PARTICIPLE OR CLAUSE: tells a method or manner of accomplishing the action in the main clause (4.6.3.8.).

MEANS (CIRCUMSTANTIAL) PARTICIPLE OR CLAUSE: tells a means of accomplishing the action in the main clause (4.6.3.7.)

MICROSTRUCTURE: analysis of syntactical patterns in a particular sentence and the smaller segments within that sentence (6 introduction)

MODAL PARTICIPLE: (circumstantial) same as manner participle (4.6.3.8.)

MODE: same as mood (4 introduction)

MOOD: that portion of a verb's meaning that tells about the actuality or potentiality of the action (4 introduction)

MORPHEME: any word or part of a word that carries some meaning (1.1.3.)

NARRATIVE PATTERN: the literary shape of a historical or fictional account; discovered by seeking answers to certain kinds of questions (6.2; 6.2.1.)

NEGATIVE: a word, phrase or clause that denies rather than asserts something (2.4.2; 4.7.2.1–2.)

NOUN: a word that names a person, place or thing (1.1.2.2.)

NOUN COMPLEMENT INFINITIVE: an infinitive that completes the meaning of a noun (4.5.2.)

OBJECT COMPLEMENT: a noun that renames the direct object in certain sentences (1.2.2.6.)

OBJECT COMPLEMENT PARTICIPLE: a participle that describes an action which is performed by the direct object of a sentence and which is perceived by the subject of that sentence (4.6.1.)

OBJECTIVE GENITIVE: a genitive noun that indicates the recipient (= object) of the action implied in the noun modified (5.1.3.)

OPTATIVE MOOD: the mood for speech and writing indicating that the action of the verb expresses a wish or hope of some sort (4.3.)

OVERLAPPING RELATIONS: in word study, words that mean the same thing in a particular context; for example in English, *beautiful* and *pretty* (6.5.5.).

PARAGRAPH: a group of sentences related by theme (1.3.)

PARAGRAPH FLOW: a visual layout of a paragraph of text (2.1.)

PARTICIPLE: in Greek, a word that is part verb and part adjective; considered a near mood or partial mood (4.6.)

PARTICLE: a short Greek word that intensifies speech (1.1.2.1.)

PARTICULARIZATION: the compositional pattern of moving from a general statement to specific examples or illustrations (6.3.7.)

PARTITIVE GENITIVE: a genitive noun that tells the entire portion from which part has been taken or designated (5.1.5.)

PASSIVE VERB: a verb in which the subject receives the action rather than doing the action (1.2.3.3.)

PERFECT TENSE: an important Greek tense that carries the idea of completed action with ongoing results; more accurately called the present perfect because the effects last into the present (3.3 and following subsections)

PERICOPE (puh-RICK-oh-pea): originally a lection or selection for public reading of Scripture; a group of sentences and paragraphs in a narrative text that tells a complete story (1.3.1.)

PERIPHRASTIC: a Greek verb phrase made up usually of a form of εἰμί plus a participle; uses two words when one would have done (3.2.1; 3.3.1, 3.4; 3.5; 3.6; 4.6.4.)

PERMISSION IMPERATIVE: use of the Greek third person imperative; usually involves an English translation *let him ___* or *let them___* (4.4.2.2.)

PLACE GENITIVE: a genitive form that answers the question *where* (5.2.1.)

PLUPERFECT TENSE: a Greek tense that carries the idea of completed action with results continuing as far as some past time; more colloquially called the past perfect (3.6 and following subsections)

POLYSEMY: multiple meanings for an individual word (6.5.2.)

POSSESSIVE GENITIVE: a genitive case noun or pronoun identifying the owner of the noun modified (5.1.1.)

PREDICATE: the verb and all the rest of a sentence except for the subject and its modifiers (1.2.2.2.)

PREDICATE ADJECTIVE: an adjective that describes the subject of a sentence that has a "be" verb (1.2.2.5.)

PREDICATE NOMINATIVE: a noun that renames the subject of a sentence that has a "be" verb (1.2.2.5.)

PREDICTIVE FUTURE: in the indicative mood a future tense verb that predicts that an action or event will occur at some future point; the main usage of the future (3.4.1.)

PREFIX: a meaning component placed before the stem of a word (1.1.3.)

PREPOSITION: a word showing the relationship of a noun, pronoun, or other substantive to the rest of a sentence (1.1.2.2.)

PREPOSITIONAL PHRASE: a group of words preceded by a preposition and without a finite verb (1.2.1.2.)

PRESENT TENSE: an important Greek tense that carries the idea of action occurring over a period of time (3.2 and following subsections)

PROCESS PRESENT: outside the indicative mood a present tense verb that tells of an action which happens over a period of time without regard to whether the action is past, present, or future (3.2.3.)

PROGRESSION: the compositional pattern of logical, step-by-step forward movement to an argument (6.3.11.)

PROHIBITION IMPERATIVE: use of μή followed by a second person present imperative verb; typically indicates that an action underway should be stopped (4.4.2.1.)

PROHIBITION SUBJUNCTIVE: use of μή followed by a second person aorist subjunctive verb; typically prohibits even beginning an action (4.2.1.2.)

PRONOUN: a word that substitutes for a noun (1.1.2.2.)

PROPHETIC FUTURE: same as predictive future (3.4.1.)

PROTASIS: the *if* part of a conditional sentence (4.1.2.3; 4.2.2.4; 4.4.2.4; 4.6.3.5.)

PROVERBIAL PRESENT, FUTURE, OR AORIST: in the indicative mood tells a general truth valid for all times (3.1.2.1; 3.2.2.2; 3.4.2.1.)

PUNCTILIAR PRESENT: in the indicative mood use of a present tense verb that tells of an action which happens at one point in the present time; a kind of descriptive present (3.2.1.)

PURE PERFECT: the usual sense of the perfect tense; notes a completed action with an effect lasting to the present time (3.3.1.)

PURE PLUPERFECT: the usual sense of the pluperfect tense; notes a completed action with an effect lasting to some past time (3.6.1.)

PURPOSE PARTICIPLE: (circumstantial) used in a dependent clause to tell the purpose of the action in the main clause (4.6.3.2.)

PURPOSE INFINITIVE OR SUBJUNCTIVE: used in a dependent clause to tell the purpose of the action in the main clause (4.2.2.1; 4.5.4.1.)

RADIATION: the compositional "pattern" of loosely tying together material around a theme (6.3.12.)

REFERENT: in word study, the thing which is in the world, outside the realm of language, to which a word refers (6.5.4.)

RELATIONAL GENITIVE: a genitive noun or pronoun identifying a personal connection, such as friendship or kinship, with the noun modified (5.1.1.)

RELATIVE PRONOUN: one way to connect a dependent clause to a sentence; in Greek, forms of ὅς and ὅστις (2.2.3.2.)

REPETITION: a compositional pattern that shows emphasis by repeating words or phrases (2.4.1; 6.3.2.)

REQUEST IMPERATIVE: use of the imperative often by one without authority over another; makes a petition or request instead of a command (4.4.2.3.)

RESULT PARTICIPLE, INFINITIVE, OR SUBJUNCTIVE: (circumstantial) used in a dependent clause to tell the result of the action in the main clause (4.2.2.2; 4.5.4.2; 4.6.3.3.)

RHETORICAL QUESTION: a question that speakers ask when they already know the answer (4.2.1.4.)

SEMANTIC FIELD (DOMAIN): the broad meaning concept within which the sense of a particular word in context is to be understood (6.5.3; 6.4.2.)

SENSE: in word study, the mental content that comes to mind upon hearing or reading a word (1.1.1; 6.5.4.)

SEPARATION GENITIVE: a genitive noun that implies physical or logical removal from the noun modified

SIMPLE AORIST: in the indicative mood tells unspecified action in past time; outside the indicative tells unspecified action without regard to time (3.1.1; 3.1.3.)

SIMPLE SENTENCE: a sentence with only one main clause and no dependent clauses (1.2.1.1.)

SIMULTANEOUS ACTION: action that happens at the same time as some other action (4.5.4.4.)

SOURCE GENITIVE: a genitive noun or pronoun indicating the origin or derivation of the noun modified (5.1.2.)

STANZA: a group of poetry lines related by theme (1.3.1.)

STATEMENT INDICATIVE: the ordinary use of the indicative mood to assert some action as real (4.1.1.)

STEM: the basic meaning component of a word (1.1.3.)

STRUCTURE MARKER: a preposition, relative pronoun, coordinate conjunction, or subordinate conjunction; so called because they relate parts of a speaker's thoughts to each other (2.2.3; 2.2.3.1–4.)

SUBJECT: who or what a sentence or narrative is about (1.2.2.1; 6.2.1.)

SUBJECT COMPLEMENT: words that complete (= complement) the subject of a sentence; a predicate nominative or a predicate adjective (1.2.2.5.)

SUBJECT COMPLEMENT PARTICIPLE: a participle that describes the subject of a sentence following a form of εἰμί; a participle used as a predicate adjective (4.6.1.)

SUBJECT OF AN INFINITIVE: the use of an accusative noun or pronoun to indicate who is doing the action of an infinitive; technically called an accusative of general reference (4.5.4.3.)

SUBJECTIVE GENITIVE: a genitive noun indicating the origin or Instigator (– subject) of the action implied in the noun modified (5.1.2.)

SUBJUNCTIVE MOOD: the mood for speech and writing that indicates that the action of the verb is uncertain or potential (4.2.)

SUBORDINATE CONJUNCTION: a word that joins a dependent clause to the rest of a sentence, for example ὅτι or ἵνα (1.2.1.3; 2.2.3.4.)

SUBSEQUENT ACTION: action that happens in time after some other action (4.5.4.4.)

SUBSTANTIATION: same as cause; the compositional pattern of giving the reason or grounds for an action or event (6.3.10.)

SUBSTANTIVE: any word that is a noun or fills a noun "slot" (such as a subject or a direct object) in a sentence; infinitives and participles often function as substantives (2.3.4; 4.5.1; 4.6.2.)

SUFFIX: a meaning component placed after the stem of a word (1.1.3.)

SUMMARY SENTENCE: a sentence that concludes the matter of a paragraph (1.3.2.)

SYNCHRONIC WORD STUDY: study of a word's usage at a particular point of time (6.5.1.)

SYNONYM: in word study, words that mean the same thing in a particular context; there are no absolute synonyms (6.5.5; 6.4.1.)

SYNTACTICAL WORD: the various spellings that a lexical entry may have in real written sentences (1.1.1; 6.5.4.)

SYNTAX: the organization of words within phrases, clauses, sentences, and paragraphs (2 introduction)

TENSE: that portion of a verb's meaning that tells about the time and kind of action (3 introduction)

TIME PARTICIPLE OR INFINITIVE: (circumstantial) used in a dependent clause to tell the time of the action in the main clause (4.5.4.4; 4.6.3.1.)

TIME GENITIVE: a genitive form that answers the question *when* (5.2.1.)

TRANSITIVE VERB: any verb in a sentence that has a direct object, with the action of the verb "transferred" to the direct object (1.2.3.1.)

UNMARKED MEANING: the meaning that comes to most peoples' minds when they see or hear a word without a context (1.1.1; 6.5.6.)

UNRESTRICTED PARTICIPLE OR CLAUSE: same as independent participle or clause (4.6.5.)

UNSPECIFIED AORIST: same as simple aorist (3.1.1; 3.1.3.)

USUS LOQUENDI: use in location; a word's meaning in a particular context (6.5.1.)

VERB: an action being done by or to the subject of a sentence or a condition of the subject; the most important part of a sentence (1.1.2.1; 1.2.2.2.)

VERBAL COMPLEMENT INFINITIVE OR PARTICIPLE: an infinitive or participle that completes (= complements) the meaning of a verb (4.5.3; 4.6.4.)

VOLITIONAL FUTURE: same as imperative future (3.4.2.2.)

VOLITIONAL OPTATIVE: use or the optative mood to express a wish; the main use of the optative (4.3.1.)